NTC BUSINESS BOOKS

# Publicity
# &
# Media
# Relations
# Checklists

## 59 PROVEN CHECKLISTS TO SAVE TIME, WIN ATTENTION, & MAXIMIZE EXPOSURE WITH *EVERY PUBLIC RELATIONS* & PUBLICITY CONTACT

# David R. Yale

# Publicity & Media Relations Checklists

## 59 PROVEN CHECKLISTS TO SAVE TIME, WIN ATTENTION, & MAXIMIZE EXPOSURE WITH *EVERY* PUBLIC RELATIONS & PUBLICITY CONTACT

### David R. Yale

*Printed on recyclable paper*

 NTC Business Books
a division of *NTC Publishing Group* • Lincolnwood, Illinois USA

**Library of Congress Cataloging-in-Publication Data**

Yale, David R.
    Publicity and media relations checklists : 59 proven checklists to
save time, win attention, and maximize exposure with every public
relations and publicity contact / David R. Yale.
        p.      cm.
    Includes bibliographical references.
    ISBN 0-8442-3218-1
    1. Industrial publicity.  2. Public relations.  3. Mass media and
business.     I. Title
HD59. Y32  1995
659--dc20                                         94-24246
                                                    CIP

**1997 Printing**

Published by NTC Business Books, a division of NTC Publishing Group
4255 West Touhy Avenue
Lincolnwood (Chicago), Illinois 60646-1975, U.S.A.

6 7 8 9 M L 9 8 7 6 5 4 3 2

Dedicated to my wife, Margaret White

# Table of Contents

# Contents

# Contents

# Introduction

I wrote *Publicity and Media Relations Checklists* for the seasoned publicist as well as the beginner. Checklists have always worked like magic for me. They help me step back, get an overview of the process, and then methodically fill in the details. They keep me from losing sight of the forest for the trees. And they help me remember the myriad details that are an essential part of publicity.

I think they will be just as useful to you.

The checklists in this book are interactive. They give you information as well as a framework that lets you input more facts and details, and then draw your own conclusions.

These checklists are designed to help you make essential decisions, keep track of details, organize information, create permanent documentation for your publicity materials in case they are challenged at a later date, and develop powerful strategic approaches to individual projects and your entire publicity program.

There are checklists that will help you develop a news peg, comply with Securities and Exchange Commission regulations, plan a news conference, localize a story, create the best possible video news release on a budget, handle controversy, pitch a feature story idea—and lots more.

Many of these checklists are intended to be filled out each time you do a project, while others should be filled out once and reviewed regularly. But they are all designed to make your job easier *and* get you better results.

Since this is an interactive book, I invite you to interact with me. Let me know how you're using the checklists, as well as any suggestions you have for improving the next edition. You can reach me in care of NTC Business Books, or on CompuServe at 70363,3660.

# Goal Setting and Market Analysis

Before you can create an effective, successful publicity campaign, you must know what you want to accomplish and what your capabilities and limitations are. The checklists in Part I will help you identify who needs to be involved in the approval process for each type of campaign and what objectives your campaigns need to achieve. The lists will also help you identify your audience for each product line, service, or issue, and decide on the best ways to reach that audience.

# Defining Your Authority

You must define approval processes and the exact limits of your authority in order to be a top-notch publicist. This checklist will help you approach that task in an organized manner. It's a good idea to review these arrangements and understandings periodically, and whenever there's a change in management in your organization. Finally, get your supervisor to initial this worksheet at the bottom, so you and he or she are sure you understand each other completely.

Date this checklist was filled out: _____

Review these arrangements again on: _____ (Enter this date in your appointment book.)

1. In the left-hand column, write down all the decisions you have to make as a publicist. Then check off whether you need approval from someone else, and fill in who you discussed this with.

| Decision | Approval Needed | Approval Not Needed | Exceptions | Discussed With |
|---|---|---|---|---|
| Publicity priorities | _____ | _____ | _____ | _____ |
| Expenditures under $_____ | _____ | _____ | _____ | _____ |
| Expenditures over $ _____ | _____ | _____ | _____ | _____ |
| Others | | | | |
| _____ | _____ | _____ | _____ | _____ |
| _____ | _____ | _____ | _____ | _____ |
| _____ | _____ | _____ | _____ | _____ |
| _____ | _____ | _____ | _____ | _____ |

2. In the left-hand column make a list of all the types of publicity you will produce. In the other columns, list the people who will need to approve each project. If you have multiple products and services with different approvals needed for each, you can photocopy this checklist and complete it for each product or service.

| Type of Publicity | Approval Needed From | Approval Needed From | Approval Needed From |
|---|---|---|---|
| How to choose, buy or use our product or service | _____ | _____ | _____ |
| Interesting facts about our product or service | _____ | _____ | _____ |

# Defining Your Authority

| Type of Publicity | Approval Needed From | Approval Needed From | Approval Needed From |
|---|---|---|---|
| Satisfied user stories for our product or service | _____ | _____ | _____ |
| How our product or service meets the needs of consumers | _____ | _____ | _____ |
| Counteracting misconceptions about our product or service | _____ | _____ | _____ |
| Interesting facts about our industry | _____ | _____ | _____ |
| Counteracting misconceptions about our industry | _____ | _____ | _____ |
| Informing the public about issues concerning our organization | _____ | _____ | _____ |
| Informing the public about issues concerning our industry | _____ | _____ | _____ |
| Informing the public about legislation concerning our organization | _____ | _____ | _____ |
| Informing the public about legislation concerning our industry | _____ | _____ | _____ |
| Financial information about our organization | _____ | _____ | _____ |
| Publicity that could impact our stock price | _____ | _____ | _____ |
| Human interest stories about our employees | _____ | _____ | _____ |
| News about promotions and retirements | _____ | _____ | _____ |

# Defining Your Authority

| Type of Publicity | Approval Needed From | Approval Needed From | Approval Needed From |
|---|---|---|---|
| Information about careers in our organization or industry | _____ | _____ | _____ |
| Publicity for events and programs | _____ | _____ | _____ |
| Other | _____ | _____ | _____ |
| | _____ | _____ | _____ |

3.  Are there more than two levels of approval needed for your publicity?

    ☐  Yes. (This could be a problem. Publicity has to meet deadlines, and more than two levels of approval will be very time consuming. You should discuss this issue with your supervisor.

    ☐  No.

4.  Can some approval levels be bypassed in an emergency?

    ☐  Yes.

    ☐  No. (This could be a problem. In an emergency, you have to respond quickly, or the media will get information from another source, perhaps your opposition. One level of approval is an obstacle, and more than one is impossible. Ideally, you should have full authority in an emergency situation. You should discuss this issue with your supervisor.)

5.  Have you gotten agreement from your supervisor about your publicity priorities on Checklist 6?

    ☐  Yes.

    ☐  No, but I'll do that/keep trying.

6.  Can you turn down a request for publicity, based on your publicity priorities, when you and your staff are overloaded?

    ☐  Yes.

    ☐  No. Reason: _____

7.  Can you turn down a request for publicity when you believe there is no news peg involved and journalists won't be interested?

    ☐  Yes.

    ☐  No. Reason: _____

8.  Do you have a clear channel to the top person in your organization, so you can get the information and approvals you need quickly?

    ☐  Yes.

    ☐  No. Reason: _____

9. Are you involved in the marketing department's strategy sessions?

☐ Yes.

☐ No. Reason: _____

10. Make a list of the information you need to do your job. If the information you're getting is inadequate, write down the action you need to take to remedy the situation.

| Information | From Department | Adequate | Inadequate | Action Needed | Action Taken |
| --- | --- | --- | --- | --- | --- |
| _____ | _____ | _____ | _____ | _____ | _____ |
| _____ | _____ | _____ | _____ | _____ | _____ |
| _____ | _____ | _____ | _____ | _____ | _____ |
| _____ | _____ | _____ | _____ | _____ | _____ |
| _____ | _____ | _____ | _____ | _____ | _____ |
| _____ | _____ | _____ | _____ | _____ | _____ |
| _____ | _____ | _____ | _____ | _____ | _____ |

Your supervisor's initials _____  Date _____

For related worksheets, see:

Checklist #6: Setting Publicity Priorities

# 2

# Publicity Goals

Publicity is a tool to help your organization reach its goals. Being as specific as possible about your publicity objectives will produce the best results for your organization. This checklist is designed with two objectives in mind:

1.  To give you an overview of your organization's publicity goals. Since these will change over time, you ought to review and revise this checklist on a regular basis. When you look back at prior versions of the checklist, you may be amazed to see the progress you have made in meeting goals since then.

2.  To help you focus each publicity project and see where it fits into your overall publicity goals, use the completed checklist and circle the goal(s) for the project at hand in red pen.

Use the extra lines after each item to add any further information or your own comments. If you have different divisions or product lines with very different goals, you may want to fill out separate versions of this checklist for each.

☐ Date: _____

☐ Corporate Division: _____

☐ Product Line: _____

We need to (check all that apply):

☐ Inform people about how to choose, buy, and use our product or service.

_____

_____

☐ Persuade people to buy our product or service rather than the competitor's.

_____

_____

☐ Overcome resistance and convince people that they need our product or service.

_____

_____

☐ Counteract misconceptions about our product or service.

_____

_____

# Publicity Goals

- [ ] Get more customers
  - [ ] to visit our stores.
  - [ ] to visit our dealers.
  - [ ] to buy our brand at retailers.
  - [ ] to order by phone.
  - [ ] to call for appointments with sales reps.
  - [ ] Other _____

  _____

- [ ] Counteract misconceptions about our
  - [ ] organization.
  - [ ] industry.
  - [ ] product.

  _____

  _____

- [ ] Inform the public about issues concerning our
  - [ ] organization.
  - [ ] industry.
  - [ ] product.

  _____

  _____

- [ ] Get people to vote for legislation that will help our organization.

  _____

  _____

- [ ] Get people to vote against legislation that will harm our organization.

  _____

  _____

- [ ] Attract shareholders and support our stock price.

  _____

  _____

# Publicity Goals

☐ Protect our organization from frivolous lawsuits.

_____

_____

☐ Attract highly qualified

    ☐ employees.

    ☐ volunteers.

_____

_____

☐ Get people to attend an event or series of events.

_____

_____

☐ Increase attendance at or participation in our organization's programs.

_____

_____

For related worksheets, see:

Checklist #5: Using Misconceptions to Your Advantage
Checklist #6: Setting Publicity Priorities

# 3

# Targeting Your Audience

It's important to define your audience as precisely as possible so you can choose the right media to reach them. This checklist will help you describe your target group. This group may vary from product to product or between divisions, so you may need to photocopy the checklist and fill out several versions. When you have identified your target audience, you can use media directories to find out which newspapers, magazines, and broadcasters will reach it. Since the audience for a product or service may change over time, you should review and revise this checklist periodically.

Date: _____

Project name: _____

Product/service/issue: _____

Appeals to:

☐ Broad, mass audience

☐ Highly specialized audience

☐ More than one audience (list below):

_____

_____

_____

_____

_____

If you make a copy of this worksheet for each audience segment you have identified above, you will be able to target them more easily.

We need to reach this (these) audience(s) in the following geographic area(s):

☐ International (list countries):

_____

_____

_____

_____

☐ National

# Targeting Your Audience

☐ Regional (list regions): _____

_____

☐ Statewide

☐ Local audience (specify area) _____

_____

_____

The audience I want to reach is

☐ currently buying our product or service.

☐ not currently buying our product or service.

☐ in agreement with our organization's stand on the issue.

☐ undecided about our organization's stand on the issue.

☐ opposed to our organization's stand on the issue, but willing to engage in a dialogue.

Age:
| | | | |
|---|---|---|---|
| ☐ Under 12 | ☐ 13–18 | ☐ 19–25 | ☐ 26–35 |
| ☐ 36–50 | ☐ 50–65 | ☐ over 65 | |

Income:
| | | |
|---|---|---|
| ☐ $10,000 or less | ☐ $10,001–$20,000 | ☐ Over $250,000 |
| ☐ $20,001–$50,000 | ☐ $50,001–$75,000 | |
| ☐ $75,001–$100,000 | ☐ $100,001–$250,000 | |

Characteristics:
| | | |
|---|---|---|
| ☐ Blue collar | ☐ White collar | ☐ Executives |
| ☐ Business owners | ☐ Salespeople | ☐ Professionals |
| ☐ Homeowners | ☐ Renters | ☐ Parents |
| ☐ Male | ☐ Female | |
| ☐ Married | ☐ Single | |
| ☐ Grandparents | ☐ Other: _____ | |

Does this product/service appeal to any particular ethnic group? (If yes, check your media directories to see if you can target this audience through ethnic media.)

☐ Yes (list) _____

_____

☐ No

# Targeting Your Audience

Does your target audience have any special interests? (If yes, check your media directories to see if you can target this audience through special interest media.)

☐ Yes (list) _____

_____

☐ No

☐ I don't know, but it's possible to find out by

    ☐ asking our sales staff.

    ☐ doing a survey.

    ☐ Other _____

For related worksheets, see:

Checklist #4: Motivating Your Audience

# Motivating Your Audience

The ultimate goal of publicity is to get people to take action: Buy your product; use your service; or change their attitudes and write their representative about issues that are critical to your organization. The more you think about how you can motivate them to take the action you want, the more effective your publicity will be.

You should fill out a copy of this worksheet for every publicity project, even if you've done one for a particular product or service before. In a new situation, you may uncover different motivational factors, particularly if the audience has changed since the previous project.

Keep this checklist in front of you as you write your publicity material. Circle the benefits you have included with a green marker. When you have finished writing, look for benefits you haven't circled. If they are important, rework your material to fit them in.

Date: _____

Product/service name: _____

Project name: _____

Audience: _____

Check the benefits that may apply to this product or service, even if you're not sure how they apply at this point.

☐ Saves time          ☐ Saves money

☐ Easier to use        ☐ More fun to use than alternatives

☐ Safer than alternatives       ☐ Higher quality results than alternatives

☐ Makes people happier       ☐ Makes people healthier

☐ Protects people's well-being    ☐ Gives people a sense of status

☐ Good for the environment     ☐ Makes buyers more attractive

☐ Other _____     ☐ Other _____

☐ Other _____     ☐ Other _____

☐ Other _____     ☐ Other _____

Write a concise benefits statement by adding five words or less to one of the two sentences below:

☐ This is the product or service that does _____ for you.

or

# Motivating Your Audience

☐ This is the product or service that makes you _____ .

In the left-hand column, list what people need to know to choose your product/service—what's involved in deciding on sizes, model numbers, options, features, and similar information. In the right-hand column, come up with a benefit based on that information.

| Need to know | Benefit |
| --- | --- |
| | |
| | |
| | |
| | |
| | |
| | |

For related worksheets, see:

Checklist #3: Targeting Your Audience
Checklist #5: Using Misconceptions to Your Advantage

# Using Misconceptions to Your Advantage

Your first reaction to misconceptions about your organization, product, service, industry, or cause may well be annoyance or anger. That's natural, but it's not helpful to you in the long run. Misconceptions tell you exactly what people need to know about you, and you can use them as the basis for a powerful publicity campaign. Since public misconceptions (and your knowledge of them) change over time, you should review this worksheet periodically. It will help you to:

1. Identify misconceptions

2. Pinpoint the facts that will counter those misconceptions

3. Turn these facts into benefits

Date: _____

The public may have misconceptions about many different aspects of your business. Make photocopies of this worksheet, and use a separate copy for each type of misconception:

☐ Our organization     ☐ Our industry     ☐ Our cause

☐ Our stock     ☐ Our product (specify): _____

☐ Other (specify): _____

Misconceptions are so useful to publicists, you should actually seek them out. Check the following list of possible sources for misconceptions about your organization, product, service, industry, or cause, and indicate which sources you have tapped, which ones you ought to use, and which sources aren't applicable to your situation. Then use the appropriate sources to gather misconceptions so you can produce publicity materials that will counter them.

Our in-house customer-service telephone staff

☐ Used     ☐ Should use     ☐ Not applicable

Remarks: _____

Our in-house customer-service complaint file

☐ Used     ☐ Should use     ☐ Not applicable

Remarks: _____

Dealer's customer-service telephone staff

☐ Used     ☐ Should use     ☐ Not applicable

Remarks: _____

# Using Misconceptions to Your Advantage

Dealer's customer-service complaint file

☐ Used ☐ Should use ☐ Not applicable

Remarks: _____

Our sales staff

☐ Used ☐ Should use ☐ Not applicable

Remarks: _____

Wholesaler's or distributor's sales staff

☐ Used ☐ Should use ☐ Not applicable

Remarks: _____

Our service and repair staff

☐ Used ☐ Should use ☐ Not applicable

Remarks: _____

Third-party service and repair staff (specify)

☐ Used ☐ Should use ☐ Not applicable

Remarks: _____

Press clippings

☐ Used ☐ Should use ☐ Not applicable

Remarks: _____

Public surveys

☐ Used ☐ Should use ☐ Not applicable

Remarks: _____

Customer surveys

☐ Used ☐ Should use ☐ Not applicable

Remarks: _____

Non-buyer surveys

☐ Used ☐ Should use ☐ Not applicable

Remarks: _____

# Using Misconceptions to Your Advantage

Other

☐ Used    ☐ Should use    ☐ Not applicable

Remarks: _____

Other

☐ Used    ☐ Should use    ☐ Not applicable

Remarks: _____

Other

☐ Used    ☐ Should use    ☐ Not applicable

Remarks: _____

Once you have gathered misconceptions, use the space below to record them and start turning them into publicity materials.

1. List as many misconceptions as you can in the left-hand column.

2. Write down the facts people need to know to correct those misconceptions in the middle column.

3. List ways to turn these facts into benefits in the right-hand column.

| Misconception | Facts Needed to Correct | Benefit Based on Facts |
|---|---|---|
| _____ | _____ | _____ |
| _____ | _____ | _____ |
| _____ | _____ | _____ |
| _____ | _____ | _____ |
| _____ | _____ | _____ |
| _____ | _____ | _____ |
| _____ | _____ | _____ |

For related worksheets, see:

Checklist #2: Publicity Goals

# Part II

# Setting Priorities and Getting Organized

The checklists in Part II cover the planning process that must take place before you can actually create a publicity campaign. You must first establish your priorities based on the goals you set in Part I. A realistic budget is also necessary as you try to identify the best media to use for your campaign and make decisions about possible press conferences, publicity campaigns, special events, and other programs. The possibility of controversy also must be addressed, and you need to be able to evaluate the success of your efforts in this area and in the overall campaign. Setting up a survey process as you create the campaign ensures the effectiveness of the post-campaign evaluation.

# Setting Publicity Priorities

Once you have formulated your publicity goals, you can set priorities. Most organizations can generate more potential publicity material than the publicist can handle, so setting priorities will help you make the best use of your time and resources. Since your publicity priorities will change over time, you should revise this worksheet regularly. Because publicity may be more important for certain products, there is space for you to list several products or services for each type of publicity.

1. Indicate whether you are getting this type of publicity by checking the appropriate box for "Get currently," "Should work on," "Don't need," "Not a high priority, or "Not applicable."

2. Rank each type of publicity in order of importance. It's a good idea to use a pencil, because you'll probably change the ranking several times.

Date: _____

**How to choose/buy/use** _____
                           (name of product or service)

_____ Priority

☐ Get currently       ☐ Should work on

☐ Don't need          ☐ Not a high priority

☐ Not applicable

**How to choose/buy/use** _____
                           (name of product or service)

_____ Priority

☐ Get currently       ☐ Should work on

☐ Don't need          ☐ Not a high priority

☐ Not applicable

**How to choose/buy/use** _____
                           (name of product or service)

_____ Priority

☐ Get currently       ☐ Should work on

☐ Don't need          ☐ Not a high priority

☐ Not applicable

# Setting Publicity Priorities

**How to choose/buy/use** _____
(name of product or service)

_____ Priority

☐ Get currently      ☐ Should work on

☐ Don't need      ☐ Not a high priority

☐ Not applicable

**Interesting facts about** _____
(name of product or service)

_____ Priority

☐ Get currently      ☐ Should work on

☐ Don't need      ☐ Not a high priority

☐ Not applicable

**Interesting facts about** _____
(name of product or service)

_____ Priority

☐ Get currently      ☐ Should work on

☐ Don't need      ☐ Not a high priority

☐ Not applicable

**Interesting facts about** _____
(name of product or service)

_____ Priority

☐ Get currently      ☐ Should work on

☐ Don't need      ☐ Not a high priority

☐ Not applicable

**Interesting facts about** _____
(name of product or service)

_____ Priority

☐ Get currently      ☐ Should work on

☐ Don't need      ☐ Not a high priority

☐ Not applicable

# Setting Publicity Priorities

**Satisfied user stories for** _____
(name of product or service)

_____ Priority

☐ Get currently  ☐ Should work on

☐ Don't need  ☐ Not a high priority

☐ Not applicable

**Satisfied user stories for** _____
(name of product or service)

_____ Priority

☐ Get currently  ☐ Should work on

☐ Don't need  ☐ Not a high priority

☐ Not applicable

**Satisfied user stories for** _____
(name of product or service)

_____ Priority

☐ Get currently  ☐ Should work on

☐ Don't need  ☐ Not a high priority

☐ Not applicable

**Satisfied user stories for** _____
(name of product or service)

_____ Priority

☐ Get currently  ☐ Should work on

☐ Don't need  ☐ Not a high priority

☐ Not applicable

**How** _____ **meets the needs of consumers**
(name of product or service)

_____ Priority

☐ Get currently  ☐ Should work on

☐ Don't need  ☐ Not a high priority

☐ Not applicable

# Setting Publicity Priorities

**How** _____ meets the needs of consumers
      (name of product or service)

_____ Priority

☐ Get currently          ☐ Should work on

☐ Don't need             ☐ Not a high priority

☐ Not applicable

**How** _____ meets the needs of consumers
      (name of product or service)

_____ Priority

☐ Get currently          ☐ Should work on

☐ Don't need             ☐ Not a high priority

☐ Not applicable

**How** _____ meets the needs of consumers
      (name of product or service)

_____ Priority

☐ Get currently          ☐ Should work on

☐ Don't need             ☐ Not a high priority

☐ Not applicable

**Counteracting misconceptions about** _____
                              (name of product or service)

_____ Priority

☐ Get currently          ☐ Should work on

☐ Don't need             ☐ Not a high priority

☐ Not applicable

**Counteracting misconceptions about** _____
                              (name of product or service)

_____ Priority

☐ Get currently          ☐ Should work on

☐ Don't need             ☐ Not a high priority

☐ Not applicable

# Setting Publicity Priorities

**Counteracting misconceptions about** _____
(name of product or service)

_____ Priority

☐ Get currently          ☐ Should work on

☐ Don't need             ☐ Not a high priority

☐ Not applicable

**Counteracting misconceptions about** _____
(name of product or service)

_____ Priority

☐ Get currently          ☐ Should work on

☐ Don't need             ☐ Not a high priority

☐ Not applicable

**Interesting facts about our industry** _____
(specify)

_____ Priority

☐ Get currently          ☐ Should work on

☐ Don't need             ☐ Not a high priority

☐ Not applicable

**Interesting facts about our industry** _____
(specify)

_____ Priority

☐ Get currently          ☐ Should work on

☐ Don't need             ☐ Not a high priority

☐ Not applicable

**Interesting facts about our industry** _____
(specify)

_____ Priority

☐ Get currently          ☐ Should work on

☐ Don't need             ☐ Not a high priority

☐ Not applicable

# Setting Publicity Priorities

**Interesting facts about our industry** _____
(specify)

_____ Priority

☐ Get currently      ☐ Should work on

☐ Don't need      ☐ Not a high priority

☐ Not applicable

**Counteracting misconceptions about our industry**

_____ Priority

☐ Get currently      ☐ Should work on

☐ Don't need      ☐ Not a high priority

☐ Not applicable

**Informing the public about issues concerning our organization**

_____ Priority

☐ Get currently      ☐ Should work on

☐ Don't need      ☐ Not a high priority

☐ Not applicable

**Informing the public about issues concerning our industry**

_____ Priority

☐ Get currently      ☐ Should work on

☐ Don't need      ☐ Not a high priority

☐ Not applicable

**Informing the public about legislation concerning our organization**

_____ Priority

☐ Get currently      ☐ Should work on

☐ Don't need      ☐ Not a high priority

☐ Not applicable

# Setting Publicity Priorities

**Informing the public about legislation concerning our industry**

_____ Priority

☐ Get currently ☐ Should work on

☐ Don't need ☐ Not a high priority

☐ Not applicable

**Financial information about our organization**

_____ Priority

☐ Get currently ☐ Should work on

☐ Don't need ☐ Not a high priority

☐ Not applicable

**Human interest stories about our employees**

_____ Priority

☐ Get currently ☐ Should work on

☐ Don't need ☐ Not a high priority

☐ Not applicable

**News about promotions and retirements**

_____ Priority

☐ Get currently ☐ Should work on

☐ Don't need ☐ Not a high priority

☐ Not applicable

**Information about careers in our organization or industry**

_____ Priority

☐ Get currently ☐ Should work on

☐ Don't need ☐ Not a high priority

☐ Not applicable

# Setting Publicity Priorities

**Publicity for events and programs**

_____ Priority

☐ Get currently          ☐ Should work on

☐ Don't need             ☐ Not a high priority

☐ Not applicable

**Other** _____
                    (specify)
_____ Priority

☐ Get currently          ☐ Should work on

☐ Don't need             ☐ Not a high priority

☐ Not applicable

**Other** _____
                    (specify)
_____ Priority

☐ Get currently          ☐ Should work on

☐ Don't need             ☐ Not a high priority

☐ Not applicable

**Other** _____
                    (specify)
_____ Priority

☐ Get currently          ☐ Should work on

☐ Don't need             ☐ Not a high priority

☐ Not applicable

**Other** _____
                    (specify)
_____ Priority

☐ Get currently          ☐ Should work on

☐ Don't need             ☐ Not a high priority

☐ Not applicable

# Setting Publicity Priorities

You are now ready to type your list of publicity priorities in order, based on the rankings you assigned to the items in the checklist. Before you type your list, cross out types of publicity you will never use because they are too low on the priority list. Put parentheses around types of low-priority publicity you will use infrequently.

It's a good idea to go over your final list of priorities with your supervisor and ask if he or she wants to review it with his or her superiors. It's also a good idea to have your supervisor sign or initial your final list. Your organization's publicity priorities now should be clear, and you will be able to keep your workload manageable by dropping low-priority activities in favor of more important tasks.

For related worksheets, see:

Checklist #2: Publicity Goals

# 7

# Budgeting for a Publicity Project

This worksheet will help you determine the direct costs for individual publicity projects. It does not include publicity materials provided by outside suppliers, like prerecorded public service announcements, video news releases, and satellite media tours, because you'll need to get estimates from the suppliers for these.

First, fill in the costs in the list on a per unit basis. In the second column enter "e" for estimated and "a" for actual amounts. If you use actual numbers, fill in the next column to document where you got the figures. In the last column, indicate the total cost of each activity (price per unit times total number of units). If you have a formula for determining how to allocate staff and overhead costs on a per project basis, you can add that to the worksheet.

Date: _____

Product/service: _____

Project: _____

This campaign includes the following materials:

☐ Printed news release for print media

_____ Number of pages

_____ Number of copies

☐ Faxed

☐ Mailed

| Activity | Cost per Unit | Estimated or Actual | Source | Total Cost |
|---|---|---|---|---|
| Printing cost | $_____ | _____ | _____ | $_____ |
| Collating/folding cost (include cost for backgrounder sheets and other supporting materials) | $_____ | _____ | _____ | $_____ |
| Inserting/stuffing/sealing cost | $_____ | _____ | _____ | $_____ |
| Postage cost | $_____ | _____ | _____ | $_____ |
| Telephone cost for faxing (include cost for backgrounder sheets and other supporting materials) | $_____ | _____ | _____ | $_____ |
| Freelance writer's fee | $_____ | _____ | _____ | $_____ |

# Budgeting for Publicity

| Activity | Cost per Unit | Estimated or Actual | Source | Total Cost |
|---|---|---|---|---|
| Cost of envelopes | $_____ | _____ | _____ | $_____ |
| Other _____ | $_____ | _____ | _____ | $_____ |
| Other _____ | $_____ | _____ | _____ | $_____ |

☐ Printed news release for broadcast

_____ Number of pages

_____ Number of copies

☐ Faxed

☐ Mailed

| Activity | Cost per Unit | Estimated or Actual | Source | Total Cost |
|---|---|---|---|---|
| Printing cost | $_____ | _____ | _____ | $_____ |
| Collating/folding cost (include cost for backgrounder sheets and other supporting materials) | $_____ | _____ | _____ | $_____ |
| Inserting/stuffing/sealing cost | $_____ | _____ | _____ | $_____ |
| Postage cost | $_____ | _____ | _____ | $_____ |
| Telephone cost for faxing (include cost for backgrounder sheets and other supporting materials) | $_____ | _____ | _____ | $_____ |
| Freelance writer's fee | $_____ | _____ | _____ | $_____ |
| Cost of envelopes | $_____ | _____ | _____ | $_____ |
| Other _____ | $_____ | _____ | _____ | $_____ |
| Other _____ | $_____ | _____ | _____ | $_____ |

☐ Backgrounder sheet(s)

_____ Number of pages

_____ Number of copies

# Budgeting for Publicity

| Activity | Cost per Unit | Estimated or Actual | Source | Total Cost |
|---|---|---|---|---|
| Printing cost | $_____ | _____ | _____ | $_____ |
| Freelance writer's fee | $_____ | _____ | _____ | $_____ |
| Other _____ | $_____ | _____ | _____ | $_____ |
| Other _____ | $_____ | _____ | _____ | $_____ |

☐ Feature story pitch

_____ Number of pages

_____ Number of copies

| Activity | Cost per Unit | Estimated or Actual | Source | Total Cost |
|---|---|---|---|---|
| Printing cost | $_____ | _____ | _____ | $_____ |
| Collating/folding cost (include cost for backgrounder sheets and other supporting materials) | $_____ | _____ | _____ | $_____ |
| Inserting/stuffing/scaling cost | $_____ | _____ | _____ | $_____ |
| Postage cost | $_____ | _____ | _____ | $_____ |
| Cost of envelopes | $_____ | _____ | _____ | $_____ |
| Freelance writer's fee | $_____ | _____ | _____ | $_____ |
| Other _____ | $_____ | _____ | _____ | $_____ |
| Other _____ | $_____ | _____ | _____ | $_____ |

☐ Printed public service announcements for live copy

_____ Number of pages

_____ Number of copies

| Activity | Cost per Unit | Estimated or Actual | Source | Total Cost |
|---|---|---|---|---|
| Printing cost | $_____ | _____ | _____ | $_____ |

# Budgeting for Publicity

| Activity | Cost per Unit | Estimated or Actual | Source | Total Cost |
|---|---|---|---|---|
| Collating/folding cost (include cost for backgrounder sheets and other supporting materials) | $_____ | _____ | _____ | $_____ |
| Inserting/stuffing/sealing cost | $_____ | _____ | _____ | $_____ |
| Postage cost | $_____ | _____ | _____ | $_____ |
| Cost of envelopes | $_____ | _____ | _____ | $_____ |
| Other _____ | $_____ | _____ | _____ | $_____ |
| Other _____ | $_____ | _____ | _____ | $_____ |

☐ Press conference/special event invitations

_____ Number of pages

_____ Number of copies

☐ Faxed

☐ Mailed

| Activity | Cost per Unit | Estimated or Actual | Source | Total Cost |
|---|---|---|---|---|
| Printing cost | $_____ | _____ | _____ | $_____ |
| Collating/folding cost (include cost for backgrounder sheets and other supporting materials) | $_____ | _____ | _____ | $_____ |
| Inserting/stuffing/sealing cost | $_____ | _____ | _____ | $_____ |
| Postage cost | $_____ | _____ | _____ | $_____ |
| Telephone cost for faxing (include cost for backgrounder sheets and other supporting materials) | $_____ | _____ | _____ | $_____ |
| Cost of envelopes | $_____ | _____ | _____ | $_____ |
| Other _____ | $_____ | _____ | _____ | $_____ |
| Other _____ | $_____ | _____ | _____ | $_____ |

# Budgeting for Publicity

☐ Media kit

_____ Number of pages

Special Folder ☐ Yes ☐ No

Items included: _____

_____

| Activity | Cost per Unit | Estimated or Actual | Source | Total Cost |
|---|---|---|---|---|
| Printing cost for item: _____ | $_____ | _____ | _____ | $_____ |
| Printing cost for item: _____ | $_____ | _____ | _____ | $_____ |
| Printing cost for item: _____ | $_____ | _____ | _____ | $_____ |
| Printing cost for item: _____ | $_____ | _____ | _____ | $_____ |
| Printing cost for item: _____ | $_____ | _____ | _____ | $_____ |
| Collating/folding cost (include cost for backgrounder sheets and other supporting materials) | $_____ | | _____ | $_____ |
| Inserting/stuffing/sealing cost | $_____ | _____ | _____ | $_____ |
| Postage cost | $_____ | _____ | _____ | $_____ |
| Cost of envelopes | $_____ | _____ | _____ | $_____ |
| Freelance writer's fee | $_____ | _____ | _____ | $_____ |
| Other _____ | $_____ | _____ | _____ | $_____ |
| Other _____ | $_____ | _____ | _____ | $_____ |

☐ Journalist feedback postcards

☐ Prestamped ☐ Unstamped

| Activity | Cost per Unit | Estimated or Actual | Source | Total Cost |
|---|---|---|---|---|
| Printing cost | $_____ | _____ | _____ | $_____ |
| Postage cost | $_____ | _____ | _____ | $_____ |

# Budgeting for Publicity

| Activity | Cost per Unit | Estimated or Actual | Source | Total Cost |
|---|---|---|---|---|
| Other _____ | $_____ | _____ | _____ | $_____ |

☐ Photos (specify number for each)

_____ Black-and-white glossies

    _____ 5 × 7   _____ 8 × 10   _____ Other size: _____

_____ Color glossies

    _____ 5 × 7   _____ 8 × 10   _____ Other size: _____

_____ Color slides

| Activity | Cost per Unit | Estimated or Actual | Source | Total Cost |
|---|---|---|---|---|
| Photographer's fee | $_____ | _____ | _____ | $_____ |
| Film cost | $_____ | _____ | _____ | $_____ |
| Proofs | $_____ | _____ | _____ | $_____ |
| Retouching/cropping/ developing cost | $_____ | _____ | _____ | $_____ |
| Multiple copies cost | $_____ | _____ | _____ | $_____ |
| Printing captions cost | $_____ | _____ | _____ | $_____ |
| Cost of cardboard/envelopes | $_____ | _____ | _____ | $_____ |
| Postage cost | $_____ | _____ | _____ | $_____ |
| Other | $_____ | _____ | _____ | $_____ |
| Other | $_____ | _____ | _____ | $_____ |
| Total direct costs | | | | $_____ |
| Staff costs (if you know how to allocate them) | | | | $_____ |
| Overhead costs (if you know how to allocate them) | | | | $_____ |
| Total costs | | | | $_____ |

# Budgeting for Publicity

Estimated number of readers/viewers _____

Divide total costs by estimated number of readers/viewers to get cost per reader/viewer _____

For related worksheets, see:

Checklist #2:  Publicity Goals
Checklist #6:  Setting Publicity Priorities

# Selecting the Right Media Outlets

Once you have targeted your audience, you need to determine the best media outlets for reaching it. This worksheet will help you examine the possibilities and make the best decisions. You should use this checklist for each publicity project you work on, even if you use a press release distribution service. A distribution service may not think of some highly targeted and critically important media outlets that seem obvious to you. If you identified two or more separate audiences in Checklist #3: Targeting Your Audience, you should fill out a separate worksheet for each of them. Use this checklist in conjunction with your media directories, and write down the names of specific media on the lines provided.

Date: _____

Product/service: _____

Project: _____

Audience: _____

This audience is:

☐ General

☐ Specific and targeted:

    ☐ Local only   ☐ Regional   ☐ National   ☐ International

This audience can be best reached through:

☐ *Mass media*

    ☐ Network television

    _____

    _____

    ☐ Network radio

    _____

    _____

    ☐ Mass circulation magazines

    _____

    _____

    ☐ Big-city daily newspapers

    _____

    _____

# Selecting the Right Media

☐ Surburban daily and weekly newspapers

_____

_____

☐ Wire services

_____

_____

☐ Syndicates and columnists

_____

_____

☐ *Specialized consumer media*

   ☐ Special-interest television programs:

      ☐ Broadcast    ☐ Cable

_____

_____

   ☐ Special-interest radio programs:

      ☐ National    ☐ Local

_____

_____

   ☐ Special-interest consumer magazines

_____

_____

   ☐ Specialized columnists:

      ☐ National    ☐ Local

_____

_____

☐ *Specialized business media*

   ☐ Business-oriented television programs:

      ☐ National    ☐ Local

_____

_____

# Selecting the Right Media

☐ Business-oriented radio shows:

    ☐ National   ☐ Local

_____

_____

☐ National business newspapers, mass circulation

_____

_____

☐ National business magazines, mass circulation

_____

_____

☐ Trade magazines

_____

_____

☐ Business columnists

_____

_____

☐ Newsletters

_____

_____

☐ Other (specify):

_____

_____

For related worksheets, see:

Checklist 3: Targeting Your Audience

# 9

# Evaluating Publicity Programs with Surveys

Surveys can help you evaluate the impact of your publicity campaigns by measuring the public's knowledge of specific facts before and after a campaign. This worksheet will help you organize the information you need to plan your surveys.

Date: _____

Product/service: _____

Project: _____

1.  In the left-hand column, list the facts that people need to know about your product or service from Checklist #5: Using Misconceptions to Your Advantage. Formulate questions based on these facts and enter them in the right-hand column.

| Fact | Survey Question(s) |
| --- | --- |
| _____ | _____ |
| _____ | _____ |
| _____ | _____ |
| _____ | _____ |
| _____ | _____ |
| _____ | _____ |
| _____ | _____ |
| _____ | _____ |

2.  List the additional information people need to know about your product or service from the Checklist #4: Motivating Your Audience. Formulate questions based on these facts and enter them in the right-hand column.

| Information | Survey Question(s) |
| --- | --- |
| _____ | _____ |
| _____ | _____ |
| _____ | _____ |
| _____ | _____ |
| _____ | _____ |

_____    _____

_____    _____

3. Add other possible questions below.

_____

_____

_____

_____

_____

_____

_____

4. Circle the most important questions in the first three sections and enter the number of questions you circled here: _____ Will you be able to ask someone these questions in two to four minutes? If not, you should cut the number of questions so you can. This is especially important for in-person and telephone surveys, because you'll lose many people if you run longer than four minutes. This also applies to mail surveys; many people won't spend more than a few minutes on a survey.

5. Simplify the questions to make them short and concise. Write the final version of your questions below.

_____

_____

_____

_____

_____

_____

_____

6. Can you ask each question in 10 seconds or less?

   ☐ Yes   ☐ No (Rewrite them so you can.)

7. Does each question ask for a specific answer?

   ☐ Yes   ☐ No (Rewrite them so they do, but see question 8 first!)

8. Have I included one question that allows for an unstructured response?

   ☐ Yes ☐ No (Rewrite one so it does.)

9. Do each of the questions focus on only one topic?

   ☐ Yes ☐ No (Rewrite them so they do.)

10. What is your target audience?

    ☐ Customers ☐ Noncustomers

    Why have you chosen this group(s)? _____

    _____

11. Write down the characteristics of your target audience (for example, age, sex, income bracket, ethnicity). If you are looking for a cross section of the population, fill in the quotas for each category, so your interviewers will be sure to get a balanced sampling. For age bracket, for example, you might set quotas for ages 18 to 24, 25 to 30, 31 to 35, 36 to 40, 40 to 50 and 51 plus.

    Characteristic: _____

    _____ quota: _____

    _____ quota: _____

    _____ quota: _____

    _____ quota: _____

    _____ quota: _____

    _____ quota: _____

    Characteristic: _____

    _____ quota: _____

    _____ quota: _____

    _____ quota: _____

    _____ quota: _____

    _____ quota: _____

    _____ quota: _____

    Characteristic: _____

    _____ quota: _____

    _____ quota: _____

    _____ quota: _____

_____ quota: _____

_____ quota: _____

_____ quota: _____

Characteristic: _____

_____ quota: _____

_____ quota: _____

_____ quota: _____

_____ quota: _____

_____ quota: _____

_____ quota: _____

Characteristic: _____

_____ quota: _____

_____ quota: _____

_____ quota: _____

_____ quota: _____

_____ quota: _____

_____ quota: _____

Characteristic: _____

_____ quota: _____

_____ quota: _____

_____ quota: _____

_____ quota: _____

_____ quota: _____

_____ quota: _____

12. How many people do you plan to survey? _____

13. How will this survey be done?

   ☐ By telephone   ☐ In person   ☐ By mail

14. How long will it take your staff or an outside service to do each survey? Be sure to allow time for finding someone willing to participate for telephone and in-person surveys. _____ minutes

15. How many people will you need to do this survey? _____

16. Can your staff do it?

    ☐ Yes, we have enough staff time.

    ☐ No, we need an outside service or temporaries.

17. Have you scheduled surveys before and after your publicity campaign?

    ☐ Yes

    ☐ No (Reevaluate your decision so you can make a meaningful comparison of before and after results.)

18. Are the questions on the before and after surveys exactly the same?

    ☐ Yes

    ☐ No (Change them so you can make a meaningful comparison of before and after results.)

For related worksheets, see:

Checklist #4: Motivating Your Audience
Checklist #5: Using Misconceptions to Your Advantage

# 10

# Planning for Controversy

Handling controversy is always difficult, but it can be rewarding and productive if you've prepared ahead of time. On the other hand, saying "no comment" or refusing to respond to a media controversy can do a great deal of damage. If you refuse to comment, journalists will almost certainly go to your opposition. This worksheet gives you a way to prepare for controversy in advance. First, make a list of all the possible controversial issues that could apply to your organization, then use this worksheet to evaluate each of them. You should put your controversy worksheets into a folder or binder, so they'll be ready the moment you need them.

Date: _____

Issue: _____

1. Describe the potential for controversy:

   _____

   _____

   _____

   _____

2. What facts and figures can you use to respond to an attack quickly?

   _____

   _____

   _____

   _____

3. Where is additional information on this topic filed? _____

4. List all the leading, difficult, tricky, and nasty questions reporters could ask you about this controversial situation. Write out your answers, show them to your organization's lawyer, and rewrite them based on his or her advice. Always avoid restating misleading or wrong information. Keep your statements positive and focused on the facts.

   Question: _____

   Answer: _____

   Rewrite based on lawyer's advice: _____

   _____

# Planning for Controversy

Question: _____

Answer: _____

Rewrite based on lawyer's advice: _____

_____

Question: _____

Answer: _____

Rewrite based on lawyer's advice: _____

_____

(Note: Make copies of this section for additional questions if necessary.)

5. Are there any aspects of this issue your lawyer forbids you to talk about with the press?

- _____

- _____

- _____

- _____

6. Is the press
   - ☐ likely to favor your position in this controversy?
   - ☐ likely to take a stand against you in this controversy?
   - ☐ neutral in this controversy and willing to listen?
   - ☐ Why? _____

   _____

7. Who are your potential allies on this issue? If you're not sure, you may want to approach other organizations in your industry or professional and trade associations to get a sense of where they stand now. List your most powerful, useful allies first.

   Name: _____

   Why are they potential allies? _____

   Contact person/phone number: _____

   Name: _____

   Why are they potential allies? _____

   Contact person/phone number: _____

# Planning for Controversy

Name: _____

    Why are they potential allies? _____

    Contact person/phone number: _____

Name: _____

    Why are they potential allies? _____

    Contact person/phone number: _____

Name: _____

    Why are they potential allies? _____

    Contact person/phone number: _____

Name: _____

    Why are they potential allies? _____

    Contact person/phone number: _____

8. Which organizations or individuals are likely to attack you or be your enemies in a controversy on this issue? Do they have any hidden motives you could expose that would discredit them?

Name: _____

    Why are they enemies? _____

    Hidden motives: _____

Name: _____

    Why are they enemies? _____

    Hidden motives: _____

Name: _____

    Why are they enemies? _____

    Hidden motives: _____

Name: _____

    Why arc they enemies? _____

    Hidden motives: _____

Name: _____

    Why are they enemies? _____

# Planning for Controversy

Hidden motives: _____

Name: _____

    Why are they enemies? _____

    Hidden motives: _____

9. Will the controversy go away on its own; should you ignore it?

    ☐ Yes   ☐ No

    ☐ Why or why not? _____

10. Will a response only serve to fuel the fires or reinforce wrong information?

    ☐ Yes   ☐ No

    ☐ Why or why not? _____

11. How can you make it look like *you're* the initiator of the debate, even if you have been attacked?

_____

_____

12. Have you discussed your organization's stance on this issue with the top executives?

Date _____ Executive's Name _____

Organization's stance: _____

_____

_____

_____

Problems with this stance: _____

_____

_____

Problem resolutions: _____

_____

_____

_____

Date _____ Executive's Name _____

Organization's stance: _____

# Planning for Controversy

_____

_____

_____

Problems with this stance: _____

_____

_____

Problem resolutions: _____

_____

_____

_____

Date _____ Executive's Name _____

Organization's stance: _____

_____

_____

_____

Problems with this stance: _____

_____

_____

Problem resolutions: _____

_____

_____

_____

For related worksheets, see:

Checklist #1:  Defining Your Authority
Checklist #2:  Publicity Goals
Checklist #5:  Using Misconceptions to Your Advantage
Checklist #57: Protecting Yourself
Checklist #59: Withstanding Public Scrutiny

# Staffing the Telephone

Journalists work under constant deadline pressure, so you need to make it very easy for them to reach you. If you don't, they may kill what would have been a great story because someone else was easier to reach and they couldn't wait. That's why you should review your telephone arrangements on a regular basis to make sure that journalists can get through to you or leave a message and get a fast response.

Date: _____

Review these arrangements again on: _____ (Enter this date in your appointment book.)

How are phone calls from journalists handled?

☐ Phone calls from journalists are routed through the switchboard.

Reason you don't have a direct line for journalists: _____

_____

☐ Phone calls from journalists are routed to a direct line to the publicity staff. (This is the best arrangement.)

Has the switchboard operator been trained to handle calls from journalists working under deadline pressure?

☐ Yes.

☐ No. Reason: _____

☐ Doesn't apply.

Who takes messages when you are not available?

_____  _____  _____
(names of staff people)

How do they keep track of your messages? _____

Have you ever failed to get a message?

☐ Yes  ☐ No

How can you improve the message system so you always get your messages in a timely manner?

_____

_____

Have your message-takers been trained to handle calls from journalists working under deadline pressure?

☐ Yes.

☐ No. Reason: _____

# Staffing the Telephone

In an emergency, or if a journalist has a pressing deadline, can your message-takers reach you immediately?

☐ Yes. How? _____

☐ No. Reason: _____

How do you stay in touch with your office when you're in the field?

☐ Call in every _____

☐ Beeper

☐ Cellular phone

☐ Other _____

Do you call your own number on a periodic basis to monitor how journalists' calls are handled?

☐ Yes, every _____ weeks/months.

    ☐ They're handled well.

    ☐ The line(s) is (are) often busy.

    ☐ Call handling needs improvement. Explain actions needed: _____

    _____

☐ No.

If you have voice mail, have you done the following?

Recorded a message that lets journalists know you'll get back to them quickly

☐ Yes.

☐ No. Reason: _____

☐ Doesn't apply.

Included a way for journalists to let someone on your staff know when they're under deadline pressure and need a quick response

☐ Yes.

☐ No. Reason: _____

☐ Doesn't apply.

Included your beeper number in your recorded message

☐ Yes.

☐ No. Reason: _____

☐ Doesn't apply.

# 12

# Planning Press Conferences and Special Events

The most common way to get the media to visit you is by holding a press conference or special event. There is only one reason for calling a press conference rather than sending out a news release: The subject demands a question-and-answer format. If reporters want to meet and question your speaker, or actually see an event happening, inviting them to a press conference or special event is in order.

Use this worksheet every time you plan to invite the press to a press conference or special event. Keep in mind that reporters don't like press conferences or events that don't meet their needs. If they could have covered it without attending, they'll be annoyed with you for not making that possible. Limit your speakers at a press conference to short presentations of 3 to 5 minutes, so there is plenty of time for questions and answers. The entire presentation should be no longer than 10 to 20 minutes.

Date: _____

Product/service: _____

Project: _____

Purpose of this media event: _____

Brief background statement of 50 words or less:

_____

_____

_____

_____

_____

Before you set up a press conference, take a long, hard look at whether you really need the press to attend. First examine your press kit for the conference or event:

Can anything be added to this material?

☐ No, it covers everything. I don't need to invite the media to the conference or event.

☐ Yes, reporters will have questions I can't anticipate. They need to interact with speakers or see the event. I should invite them.

Can I get good coverage with one or more of the following methods?

☐ News release

☐ News photos

☐ Press kit

# Planning Press Conferences

☐ Background materials

☐ Video news release

☐ Approaching a few carefully selected reporters and developing stories directly with them

☐ Scheduling product demonstrations for one reporter at a time to allow for intensive questions and answers

☐ Other_____

    ☐ Yes. I shouldn't invite the media.

    ☐ No. I should invite the media.

Where should I hold my press conference or special event?

☐ On site because reporters will want to see the news-making scene:

    ☐ The location is easily accessible.

    ☐ The location is *not* easily accessible. I will need

        ☐ a simultaneous press conference in a more accessible location.

        ☐ a satellite media tour to bring the setting to the media (see Checklist #26).

☐ In a city that has specialized reporters who will understand the topic and give me the best possible coverage:

    ☐ Federal government issues—Washington, DC

    ☐ Financial stories—New York

    ☐ Show business—New York or Los Angeles

    ☐ Agriculture—Chicago or Washington, DC

    ☐ Other _____

    ☐ Other _____

☐ In a city where local reporters, who often set the tone for national coverage, are likely to give my story positive coverage.

**Cities with Positive Reporters (consider)**        **Cities with Negative Reporters (avoid)**

_____      _____

_____      _____

_____      _____

_____      _____

☐ In a city that has network and wire service news bureaus, so I maximize my chance to get good coverage. Check off the news bureaus for each city you're considering:

# Planning Press Conferences

| City: | ABC | CBS | NBC | CNN | PBS | AP | UPI | Reuters | Bloomberg | Other |
|-------|-----|-----|-----|-----|-----|-----|-----|---------|-----------|-------|
| _____ | ___ | ___ | ___ | ___ | ___ | ___ | ___ | ___ | ___ | ___ |
| _____ | ___ | ___ | ___ | ___ | ___ | ___ | ___ | ___ | ___ | ___ |

If I'm not holding the press conference or special event on site, I need to make sure the location is suitable for the media

☐ Central location near media offices

☐ Building that *does not* have restricted access, unless I make arrangements for the media to be admitted immediately

☐ Built-in sound and lighting systems for television coverage (or portable rented systems) give you much better control

If I'm holding the press conference or special event outdoors, I need to make these arrangements:

☐ Provisions for bad weather

☐ Lighting for nighttime events

☐ Noise control

☐ Crowd control and security

☐ Permits, if needed

Speakers

Name: _____ Length of speech: _____

Qualifications and background: _____

Main points stated in 10 to 20 seconds:

1. _____

2. _____

3. _____

Name: _____ Length of speech: _____

Qualifications and background: _____

Main points stated in 10 to 20 seconds:

1. _____

# Planning Press Conferences

2. _____

3. _____

Name: _____  Length of speech: _____

    Qualifications and background: _____

    Main points stated in 10 to 20 seconds:

1. _____

2. _____

3. _____

List every possible thing that could go wrong at this media event, along with your plan to fix it.

| Problem | Solution |
|---|---|
| _____ | _____ |
| _____ | _____ |
| _____ | _____ |
| _____ | _____ |

For related worksheets, see:

Checklist #10: Planning for Controversy
Checklist #15: Developing a News Peg or Angle
Checklist #16: Formats for Printed Publicity Material
Checklist #17: Preparing Backgrounder Sheets
Checklist #25: Invitations to Press Conferences and Special Events
Checklist #26: Planning Satellite Media Tours
Checklist #43: Journalist Contact Preferences
Checklist #44: Telephone Contact Strategy Worksheet
Checklist #50: Following Up Press Conferences and Special Events
Checklist #59: Withstanding Public Scrutiny

# 13

# Video Production Approvals

You can save a lot of time and production money by carefully arranging approvals for video production for public service announcements, video news releases, and television feature stories. Use this worksheet to map out the approval process for each video shoot.

Date: _____

Product/service: _____

Project: _____

Date of shoot: _____

Time: _____

Location: _____

Who will need to give approval before the cameras can roll for each scene at the shoot?

| | Will Attend Shoot | | |
| Name | Yes | No | Remarks |
| --- | --- | --- | --- |
| _____ | _____ | _____ | _____ |
| _____ | _____ | _____ | _____ |
| _____ | _____ | _____ | _____ |
| _____ | _____ | _____ | _____ |

Date of pre-edit viewing: _____

Time: _____

Location: _____

Who will need to view the raw footage to choose the best takes before the editing session?

| | Will Attend Pre-edit Viewing | | |
| Name | Yes | No | Remarks |
| --- | --- | --- | --- |
| _____ | _____ | _____ | _____ |
| _____ | _____ | _____ | _____ |
| _____ | _____ | _____ | _____ |
| _____ | _____ | _____ | _____ |

# Video Production Approvals

Date of editing session: _____

Time: _____

Location: _____

Who will need to give approval at each stage of the editing session?

| Name | Will Attend Editing Session | | Remarks |
| | Yes | No | |
| --- | --- | --- | --- |
| _____ | _____ | _____ | _____ |
| _____ | _____ | _____ | _____ |
| _____ | _____ | _____ | _____ |
| _____ | _____ | _____ | _____ |

For related worksheets, see:

Checklist #24: Creating the Video News Release Concept
Checklist #37: Technical Requirements for Video News Releases
Checklist #40: Public Service Announcements
Checklist #42: Getting Public Service Announcements for Businesses
Checklist #54: The Right Production House for Your Video News Release

# Part III

# Creating Publicity Materials

The checklists in this section help you create powerful publicity materials, step-by-step, from researching your topic to choosing the most powerful information from the facts you uncover, developing strong news pegs, and making sure it all fits the formats journalists need. The checklists here help you increase your publicity placement with local angles, use your organization's expertise to get coverage, and prepare backgrounder sheets for more in-depth stories.

There are checklists that will help you write and edit strong news releases, choose and supervise the right staff writer or freelancer for each project, create product publicity that meets your organization's goals *and* is irresistible to journalists, and develop invitations to press conferences and special events that get results.

Even if you've already created successful Satellite Media Tours (SMTs) and Video News Releases (VNRs), the two checklists on these topics will make your next project far easier by helping you organize the massive amount of details involved. If you're tackling your first SMT or VNR, these checklists will help you avoid many pitfalls beginners often experience and get great results.

Finally, you'll discover how to get the most mileage from your publicity materials and how you might use them to develop powerful alliances with other departments in your organization.

# Selecting Newsworthy Facts

Whether you're preparing a news release or an invitation to a press conference or special event, you need to select exciting but newsworthy facts, build a newsworthy story from those facts, and understand what type of story it is. This worksheet will help you.

1. Make sure you include newsworthy facts journalists want

2. Understand what type of story you have

You should fill out a copy of this worksheet for every news release or media event invitation you write.

Date: _____

Product/service: _____

Project: _____

## Type of News Story

☐ This is hard, breaking news that has time value and must be covered immediately or it will be stale.

☐ This is soft or (evergreen) news that has more of a human-interest angle, and will be just as usable next week or next month as it is now.

## Basic Facts

☐ Have I included *who* is doing *what* for *whom?*

☐ Have I covered *when, where,* and *why* they are doing it?

☐ Did I explain *how* it is being done?

☐ Does my story explain *what* the results are?

☐ Are there any other basic *who, when, where, what, why, what* or *how* questions I need to answer?

    ☐ Who?_____

    ☐ When?_____

    ☐ Where? _____

    ☐ Why?_____

    ☐ What? _____

    ☐ How?_____

# Selecting Newsworthy Facts

Exciting Facts

☐ *Why* is the product, service, or event exciting?

_____

_____

☐ *What* will it do for buyers or participants?

_____

_____

☐ *How* will it save them money or time?

_____

_____

☐ *Why* is it better than what's on the market now?

_____

_____

☐ *What* research was involved in developing it?

_____

_____

☐ *What* tests show its superior performance?

_____

_____

☐ *Who* is using it already?

_____

_____

☐ *What* are its specifications?

_____

_____

# Selecting Newsworthy Facts

☐ *How* was the technology discovered?

_____

_____

☐ *What* is the human story behind the product's development and use?

_____

_____

☐ *How* can I make the statistics exciting by comparing them to things that can be visualized (for example, saves enough trees to cover the city with a forest)?

_____

_____

**Compelling Opinions**

Have I backed up my opinions with verifiable facts?

☐ Yes ☐ No

Have I attributed opinions to spokespeople and placed them in quotation marks, so this reads like a news story?

☐ Yes ☐ No

Are these opinions stated in interesting, highly visual language?

☐ Yes ☐ No

Have my spokespeople taken strong, unequivocal stands on the issues?

☐ Yes ☐ No

Is my release written in the third person?

☐ Yes ☐ No

For related worksheets, see:

Checklist #15. Developing a News Peg or Angle
Checklist #17. Preparing Backgrounder Sheets
Checklist #18. Backgrounding News Stories
Checklist #20. Publicity for Products
Checklist #21. Writing and Editing News Releases
Checklist #24. Creating the Video News Release Concept
Checklist #29. Pitching Feature Stories to Newspapers and Magazines
Checklist #36. Preparing News Releases for Broadcasters

# 15 Developing a News Peg or Angle

The news peg, or angle, is the framework on which you build a news story. It's the most important thing in a news release. You can take the same set of facts and use two, three, or more news pegs to create entirely different stories. Perhaps most important, some news pegs are weak, whereas others are stronger, even with the identical facts. This checklist will help you find new and original ways to look at your product or service, industry, organization, or cause and develop possible news pegs.

Date: _____

Product/service: _____

Project: _____

1. What facts do people need to know to counter misconceptions about your product or service, industry, or cause? Choose the most interesting items from Checklist #5 and list these in the left-hand column. What can you say that's new, different, and unusual about each of these facts? Indicate this on the right. Do you see any news pegs emerging here? Circle any facts with potential.

| Fact | News Peg |
|------|----------|
|      |          |
|      |          |
|      |          |
|      |          |
|      |          |
|      |          |

2. What are the four most powerful benefits of your product or service from Checklist #4? List them in the left-hand column. In the right-hand column, indicate what you can say about them that is new, different, and unusual. Circle any potential news pegs.

| Benefit | News Peg |
|---------|----------|
|         |          |
|         |          |
|         |          |
|         |          |

# Developing a News Peg

3. What do people need to know to choose, buy, and use your product or service? List the most interesting and unusual facts you wrote on Checklist #4 in the left-hand column, and indicate anything new and different you can say about them in the right-hand column. Circle any potential news pegs.

| Fact | News Peg |
| --- | --- |
| _____ | _____ |
| _____ | _____ |
| _____ | _____ |
| _____ | _____ |
| _____ | _____ |
| _____ | _____ |

4. Can you tie this news story into any of the following?

☐ Holiday or seasonal theme. How?_____

☐ Anniversary. Which one? _____

How? _____

☐ New world record. Which one? _____

How? _____

☐ Award. Which one?_____

To whom? _____

How? _____

☐ New information on a major debate already getting media coverage. Which one? _____

How? _____

☐ An event designed mainly to get media coverage.

☐ An event designed to draw many people and get media coverage.

☐ An event designed to dramatize a controversy?

Describe event:_____

How does it tie in to your news story? _____

_____

# Developing a News Peg

5. Can you create local angle stories with

☐ Information on how your product or service is used locally?

☐ Interviews with local experts?

☐ A local twist to a story getting national media coverage?

☐ Other _____

☐ Other _____

6. Can you offer background information on a story getting national media coverage? List the information you have that is not being included in media coverage of this story.

_____

_____

_____

_____

_____

_____

7. List your best possible pegs in the left-hand column below. Then rank them from one to six, with one being the strongest, in the right-hand column below.

| Possible News Pegs | Rank |
| --- | --- |
| _____ | _____ |
| _____ | _____ |
| _____ | _____ |
| _____ | _____ |
| _____ | _____ |

For related worksheets, see:

Checklist #4. Motivating Your Audience
Checklist #5. Using Misconceptions to Your Advantage

# Formats for Printed Publicity Material

Whether you're sending out a news release or distributing material for a press conference, there are certain generalized format preferences you should follow to make sure you project a professional image that will get you journalists' consideration. Preparing your material this way also makes it easy to use, and journalists appreciate that. Once you have used this checklist for a while, it will become second nature, and you won't have to refer to it any more. You should use it along with the checklists for specialized publicity material.

• Is your material typed or printed, with nothing handwritten?

• Did you use a carbon electric typewriter ribbon or letter-quality PC printer?

• Did you stick to standard typefaces, with no script or fancy fonts?

• Are your copies clean and neat, and did you avoid carbon copies?

• Is everything on 8½" × 11", white, 20- or 24-lb. bond paper (colored paper is not considered professional in appearance)?

• Is your organization's name, contact name, address, and telephone number, as well as the date, on top of *every* sheet of paper?

• Did you use paper clips instead of staples?

• Have you mailed only one news release per envelope?

• Did you use #10 white business envelopes for releases of one to five pages?

• Did you use 9 × 12 white envelopes with green diamond first class borders for releases six pages or longer, or when sending photos?

• Did you send everything by first class mail, express mail, or overnight courier service?

For related worksheets, see:

Checklist #25: Invitations to Press Conferences and Special Events
Checklist #29: Pitching Feature Stories to Newspapers and Magazines
Checklist #30: Writing Letters to the Editor
Checklist #33: Technical Requirements for News Photos
Checklist #36: Preparing News Releases for Broadcasters

# 17 Preparing Backgrounder Sheets

You should always include a backgrounder sheet with your news releases, press conference invitations, requests for coverage, and public service announcements because it gives you credibility and helps journalists write in-depth stories about you. A good backgrounder sheet may even generate more extensive and varied coverage than you had imagined possible.

Here are the items you should include in the backgrounder sheets for nonprofit groups:

☐ Purpose of the organization

☐ When and where it was formed

☐ Who is on the Board of Directors

☐ Where it gets its funding

☐ What it has achieved

☐ Its exact tax-exempt status

☐ The amount spent on administrative overhead versus direct services

☐ Local and state registration compliance, if applicable

☐ Lobbyist status, if applicable

Here are the items you should include in backgrounder sheets for profit-making companies.

☐ Products manufactured, distributed, or sold

☐ Services rendered

☐ Unique position and achievements in the marketplace

☐ Awards, honors, or recognition your products or services have received

☐ Awards, honors, or recognition your organization has received for public service to the community

☐ Status (publicly held corporation, closely held corporation, family business, or partnership)

☐ Capitalization if you're not a Fortune 500 or Inc. 500 organization

☐ Sales volume

☐ Top officers' names

# Preparing Backgrounder Sheets

☐ The organization's name, address, and telephone number, and the contact person's name and telephone number

For related worksheets, see:

Checklist #16: Formats for Printed Publicity Material
Checklist #18: Backgrounding News Stories

# 18

# Backgrounding News Stories

You can often get publicity for your organization, products, service, cause, or industry by positioning yourself as an expert with the media, latching on to a breaking national story, and providing background information the media may not have. This can be a one-shot effort, or you can promote yourself as an expert the media can call on whenever your topic is in the news. If you do this successfully, you can run circles around your competition and become known as *the* expert on this topic.

Here's how you can position yourself as an expert on a continuing basis:

- [ ] Distribute a resource file to journalists who cover your topic
    - [ ] Use a file folder with a prelabeled tab
    - [ ] Or use a loose leaf binder with a nicely designed cover insert
    - [ ] Include factual material on your topic of expertise
    - [ ] Organize it into sections marked off by tabs
    - [ ] Include a request for attribution on the first page and the bottom of every page, so you get credit as the source of the information
    - [ ] Set up a program to update the material on a regular basis

- [ ] Set up and promote a toll-free hotline for journalists
    - [ ] Use an 800 number
    - [ ] Include your hours of operation in your material or use the latest voice mail technology to provide 24-hour access to recorded information that can be chosen from a menu
    - [ ] Tie your 800 number to a beeper service and let journalists know you're instantly available when they need in-depth consultations
    - [ ] Provide a Rolodex® card to keep your number at journalists' fingertips
    - [ ] Have an extensive, accurate database on your topic
    - [ ] Offer to research questions that go beyond your database or your current knowledge
    - [ ] Ask journalists to attribute the information to you

- [ ] Set up a toll-free bulletin board for journalists
    - [ ] Use an 800 number
    - [ ] Provide a Rolodex® card to keep your bulletin board's number at journalists' fingertips
    - [ ] Choose user-friendly, commercially available software
    - [ ] Make sure you have a search feature that's easy to use
    - [ ] Include files about the various aspects of your issue
    - [ ] Have an extensive, accurate database on your topic
    - [ ] Offer to research questions that aren't answered in the database

# Backgrounding News Stories

☐ Include a list of experts available for interviews in the database, with background information about each of them and details about how they can be reached

☐ Include a request for attribution on the welcome screen so you get credit as the source of the information.

For related worksheets, see:

Checklist #17: Preparing Backgrounder Sheets

# Increasing Publicity Placements with Local Angles

Many smaller weekly and daily papers, as well as smaller broadcasters, limit themselves to covering local news; still others prefer it. Localizing a national news release can increase your coverage as much as five times and also have more of an impact on your audience. Always mark your envelope and press release "Local Angle Story," so the journalist will know at a glance that what may seem like an out-of-town release really isn't. This worksheet will help you localize your stories. You should use it for each news release you write. Keep in mind that only about one third of the material in your release needs to be localized.

Date: _____

Product/service: _____

Project: _____

For each story you want to localize, ask yourself if you can

☐ get information from your dealers or distributors about local customers who are using your product.

☐ generate local statistics about this product or issue.

☐ attribute this announcement to different local spokespeople.

☐ refer reporters to local experts.

☐ tie localized versions of this story to the interest created by a national story on the same subject.

☐ combine these approaches for an even more powerful story.

For related worksheets, see:

Checklist #21: Writing and Editing News Releases
Checklist #23: Meeting the Needs of Broadcast Journalists
Checklist #26: Planning Satellite Media Tours
Checklist #29: Pitching Feature Stories to Newspapers and Magazines
Checklist #36: Preparing News Releases to Broadcasters
Checklist #38: Pitching Video News Releases

# Publicity for Products

There are two basic kinds of products, and each of them should be publicized differently:

- *Commodity products* are all basically the same. Your widget is basically like everyone else's widget. Commodity products are more difficult to publicize because there is usually nothing new about them. Packaged goods and personal computers are commodity products.

- *Differentiated products* have features and benefits that are different from each other. Books, some toys, and heavy industrial equipment are examples of differentiated products.

Fill in a copy of this worksheet for every product you publicize:

Date: _____

Product/service: _____

Project: _____

Check off the strategies you should consider for this product:

## Strategies that work best for commodity products

☐ Find features or benefits your competitors haven't claimed.

☐ Tie your product to an event of interest to consumers, like a race or sports tournament.

☐ Tie your product to an issue of interest to consumers, like safety or environmental concerns.

## Strategies that work for either commodity or differentiated products

☐ Address common misconceptions about your product.

☐ Teach consumers how to make buying decisions about your product.

☐ Show consumers how to use your product.

☐ Explain how your product can be used to save time or money.

Product publicity often demands that you coordinate your efforts with other departments like marketing or product management. Use this section to list with whom you have to coordinate on this project.

Name: _____ Department: _____ Extension: _____

☐ Information source only

☐ Must approve strategy

☐ Must approve copy

# Publicity for Products

☐ Should see placements

☐ Other _____

☐ Other _____

Name: _____ Department: _____ Extension: _____

☐ Information source only

☐ Must approve strategy

☐ Must approve copy

☐ Should see placements

☐ Other _____

☐ Other _____

Name: _____ Department: _____ Extension: _____

☐ Information source only

☐ Must approve strategy

☐ Must approve copy

☐ Should see placements

☐ Other _____

☐ Other _____

Name: _____ Department: _____ Extension: _____

☐ Information source only

☐ Must approve strategy

☐ Must approve copy

☐ Should see placements

☐ Other _____

☐ Other _____

# Publicity for Products

How you select and treat the facts in your news release can make a great difference. The following list can help you create an exciting, newsworthy story.

☐ What can the product do that's new and exciting?

☐ What will it do for buyers or participants?

☐ How will it save them money or time?

☐ Why is it better than what's on the market now?

☐ What research was involved in developing it?

☐ What tests show its superior performance?

☐ Who is using it already?

☐ What are its specifications?

☐ How was the technology discovered?

☐ What is the human story behind the product's development and use?

☐ How can I make the statistics exciting by comparing them to things that can be visualized (for example, saves enough trees to cover the city with a forest)?

For related worksheets, see:

Checklist #1: Defining Your Authority
Checklist #14: Selecting Newsworthy Facts
Checklist #15: Developing a News Peg or Angle
Checklist #21: Writing and Editing News Releases
Checklist #24: Creating the Video News Release Concept
Checklist #29: Pitching Feature Stories to Newspapers and Magazines
Checklist #36: Preparing News Releases for Broadcasters

# 21

# Writing and Editing News Releases

News releases are the cornerstone of your publicity program. Always keep in mind that you are competing with hundreds, and maybe even thousands, of other releases for scarce space. Since editors get so many releases, they take only a second or two to judge them. If your release looks like news, it will get further consideration; if it doesn't, it will be immediately discarded. This is why the format of your news releases is as important as their content. Use this worksheet to plan and check each release you do:

1. map out the content,

2. make sure it fits news release format, and

3. finalize your plans for distribution and supporting materials.

Since you will need a news peg before you start to write, you should fill in Checklist #15 first and refer to it as you write.

Date: _____

Product/Service: _____

Project: _____

## Contents

1. Make a list of all the points you want to cover, then prioritize them.

**Priority**    **Point**

_____    _____

_____    _____

_____    _____

_____    _____

_____    _____

_____    _____

_____    _____

_____    _____

_____    _____

_____    _____

# Writing News Releases

2. Go over your list again, checking to make sure that you have included each of the following:

- Who

- When

- Where

- Why

- How

- What

If you haven't, add the missing points now and reprioritize.

3. Write your release, with the most important point first, the second-most important point next, and so on, until you get to the last, least important point.

4. Let your release sit overnight; it will be easier to edit after you have some distance from it.

5. Check it against the editing and format sections below.

## Editing

1. Are you using short words rather than long words so the release is easy to read and understand?

2. Have you translated jargon and technical words into everyday language?

3. If you have to use one or two technical terms, have you defined them?

4. Have you cut out as many words as possible from your release, especially adjectives and the word "that"?

5. Have you avoided the passive voice?

6. Do most of your sentences use fewer than 20 words?

7. Are your paragraphs short, with an average of four to five lines?

8. Have you checked to make sure you don't have two or more paragraphs that start with the same words?

9. Have you avoided repeating the same words or phrases?

10. Have you written "ok" above any unusual spellings to let the editor know they are not misspelled?

11. If it is important for readers to call you, is your telephone number in the first or second paragraph?

# Writing News Releases

## Format

1. Is your news release neatly typed on 8½ × 11" plain white bond paper?

2. Does your release include the following points?

   - The name, address, and telephone number of your business or organization

   - The name and telephone number of the contact person

   - The date, and the words "for immediate release"

   - A brief description of any photos

3. Have you included a nighttime telephone number? Will you have someone at that number to respond to calls and answer questions?

4. Have you dated the release a day or two ahead of its estimated arrival at the editor's desk?

5. If you are asking editors to hold the release, have you included the words "for release after…" and a date?

6. Have you included a headline that summarizes the story and generates interest?

7. Have you left at least two inches blank at the top of your release, so the editor has space to edit?

8. Are the lines in your release between 50 and 60 characters long?

9. Is your entire release double-spaced?

10. Are your paragraphs indented ten spaces, which journalists prefer?

11. Have you avoided hyphenation, so each line ends with a complete word?

12. If your release runs more than one page, can you cut it or cover some material in a fact sheet or backgrounder instead?

13. If you have a two-page release, does the first page end with a complete paragraph? Have you typed "MORE" across the bottom of the page at least three times?

14. Does the second page have a heading to identify it?

15. Have you ended your release with the digits "30" or the number sign (##), which means "the end" in journalese?

## Distribution and Supporting Materials

1. How will this release be distributed?

   ☐ First class mail   ☐ Overnight courier   ☐ Fax

   ☐ Wire service   ☐ In-house   ☐ Distribution service

   ☐ Other _____

# Writing News Releases

2. What distribution lists will you use?

_____

_____

_____

3. Will you include a fact sheet or backgrounder with this release?

☐ Yes.   ☐ No, because _____

_____

4. Will you include photos with this release?

☐ Yes.   ☐ No, because _____

_____

5. Will you include other supporting materials with this release?

☐ No.   ☐ Yes, I plan to include _____

_____

For related worksheets, see:

Checklist #14: Selecting Newsworthy Facts
Checklist #15: Developing a News Peg or Angle
Checklist #16: Formats for Printed Publicity Material
Checklist #17: Preparing Backgrounder Sheets
Checklist #18: Backgrounding News Stories
Checklist #19: Increasing Publicity Placements with Local Angles
Checklist #20: Publicity for Products
Checklist #21: Writing and Editing News Releases
Checklist #22: Working with Writers
Checklist #23: Meeting the Needs of Broadcast Journalists
Checklist #36: Preparing News Releases for Broadcasters

# 22

# Working with Writers

Publicists have to work with writers, whether they're on staff; freelancers hired on a project basis; or experts, clients, and customers who volunteer to do an article. Choose the right writer, and your job will be easier and you'll increase your chances of success. The wrong writer, on the other hand, can cause incredible headaches. Use the following guidelines when choosing a writer for a publicity project.

## Options for writers:

### Staff writers

1. _____

   Advantages of using: _____

   Disadvantages of using: _____

2. _____

   Advantages of using: _____

   Disadvantages of using: _____

3. _____

   Advantages of using: _____

   Disadvantages of using: _____

### Clients/Customers

1. _____

   Advantages of using: _____

   Disadvantages of using: _____

2. _____

   Advantages of using: _____

   Disadvantages of using: _____

3. _____

   Advantages of using: _____

   Disadvantages of using: _____

# Working with Writers

**Experts**

1. _____

   Advantages of using: _____

   Disadvantages of using: _____

2. _____

   Advantages of using: _____

   Disadvantages of using: _____

3. _____

   Advantages of using: _____

   Disadvantages of using: _____

**Freelancers**

1. _____

   Advantages of using: _____

   Disadvantages of using: _____

2. _____

   Advantages of using: _____

   Disadvantages of using: _____

3. _____

   Advantages of using: _____

   Disadvantages of using: _____

## Using Freelance Writers

Writer's Name: _____

☐ I have used this writer before with satisfactory results.

☐ This is a new writer. I will do the following:

   ☐ Review his or her resumé.   Evaluation: _____

   _____

   ☐ Check his or her references.   Evaluation: _____

   _____

# Working with Writers

☐ Look at his or her portfolio.   Evaluation: _____

_____

☐ Ask him or her to suggest news pegs for this topic to see if the suggestions are on target.

News pegs suggested

1. _____

Evaluation: _____

2. _____

Evaluation: _____

3. _____

Evaluation: _____

☐ Determine that he or she understands the topic of the article by asking him or her these questions:

1. _____

Understands? _____

2. _____

Understands? _____

3. _____

Understands? _____

4. _____

Understands? _____

5. _____

Understands? _____

6. _____

Understands? _____

☐ Decide if his or her approach is interesting and exciting.

☐ Yes, it is interesting.   ☐ No, it's not interesting.

☐ Ask him or her how busy he or she is at least two different ways to make sure he or she can meet my deadlines.

# Working with Writers

1. _____

Satisfactory? _____

2. _____

Satisfactory? _____

3. _____

Satisfactory? _____

☐ Ask about his or her membership in professionals organizations. _____

☐ I have a written contract with this freelance writer that has been approved by the legal department and which specifies the following:

- This is work performed for hire.

- Our organization owns all rights to this work.

- The writer will not solicit or accept payment from the magazine.

- The writer is an independent contractor, not an employee.

- The writer will not get a byline (credit line) for this story.

☐ The writer has signed a memo of understanding (MOU) that outlines the assignment, including the following:

- The topics to be covered in the article

- The research to be performed by the writer

- Interviews to be done by the writer

- The due date for the first draft

- The writer's agreement to provide one rewrite

- The due date for the rewrite

- The fee to be paid to the writer

- Payment of one half of the writer's fee on signing the MOU

- No payment beyond the first if the first draft is not satisfactory

- Payment of one quarter of the writer's fee within five days of delivery of the first draft, unless it is unsatisfactory

- Payment of one quarter of the writer's fee within five days of delivery of the rewrite, unless it is unsatisfactory.

- A copy of the magazine's guidelines for writers

- Three to four sample copies of the magazine

- A copy of the outline for the article, including the news peg to which the editor has agreed

# Working with Writers

☐ The deadlines I have given the writer are _____ days/weeks earlier than the actual deadlines to allow for any problems or emergencies.

## Using On-Staff Writers

☐ The writer has received a memo that outlines the assignment, including the following:

- The topics to be covered in the article

- The research to be performed by the writer

- Interviews to be done by the writer

- The due date for the first draft

- The due date for the rewrite

- A copy of the magazine's guidelines for writers

- Three to four sample copies of the magazine

- A copy of the outline for the article, including the news peg the editor has agreed on.

☐ The deadlines I have given the writer are _____ days/weeks earlier than the actual deadlines to allow for any problems or emergencies

## Using Experts, Clients, and Customers as Writers

☐ I have let the expert, customer, or client know up front that

    ☐ our staff reserves the right to rewrite the article.

    ☐ he or she should provide us with notes and information, which we will use to write the article.

    ☐ he or she should make an audiotape, which we will use as the basis of the article.

☐ The expert, customer, or client has received a memo that outlines the article, including the following:

- The topics to be covered in the article

- The research to be performed or provided by the writer

- Interviews to be done by the writer

- The due date for the first draft

- The due date for the rewrite

- A copy of the outline for the article, including the news peg to which the editor has agreed

☐ The deadlines I have given the expert, customer, or client are _____ days/weeks earlier than the actual deadlines to allow for any problems or emergencies.

# 23

# Meeting the Needs of Broadcast Journalists

Broadcast journalists are under continual deadline pressure, with hourly deadlines for some radio news-casters and two or more deadlines nightly for television. They won't have much time to talk with you, and they'll have even less time to edit your material. You should prepare material that meet their needs to maximize the chances of their using it. For each station you plan to work with, use this worksheet to record needs and preferences. You'll learn these by listening to or watching the station, by consulting media directories, by talking with journalists, and from experience.

Station: _____ ☐ AM  ☐ FM  ☐ Television  ☐ Cable

Format: _____

Audience: _____

Mailing address: _____

Fax _____ Use fax for  ☐ solicited materials only
☐ unsolicited materials

News Director _____ Direct-dial line _____

News Assignment Editor _____ Direct-dial line _____

Specialized reporters:

| **Name** | **Topic** | **Direct-Dial Line** |
| --- | --- | --- |
| _____ | _____ | _____ |
| _____ | _____ | _____ |
| _____ | _____ | _____ |
| _____ | _____ | _____ |
| _____ | _____ | _____ |

News story length preferred: _____

Station uses the following:

☐  Written news releases

☐  Slides

   Mount types:  ☐ glass only   ☐ plastic   ☐ cardboard

# Needs of Broadcast Journalists

- ☐ Broadcast-quality audiocassette news releases

- ☐ Video news releases

- ☐ Satellite media tours

- ☐ Live reports by telephone

- ☐ Local news only

- ☐ National news only

- ☐ Both

News story types preferred: _____

_____

Avoid contacting this station at deadline times unless you have major, breaking news.

| Day | Name of Show | Lead Time Needed | Deadline |
|-----|-------------|------------------|----------|
| Monday | _____ | _____ | _____ |
| Tuesday | _____ | _____ | _____ |
| Wednesday | _____ | _____ | _____ |
| Thursday | _____ | _____ | _____ |
| Friday | _____ | _____ | _____ |
| Saturday | _____ | _____ | _____ |
| Sunday | _____ | _____ | _____ |

For related worksheets, see:

Checklist #36: Preparing News Releases for Broadcasters
Checklist #37: Technical Requirements for Video News Releases

# 24

# Creating the Video News Release Concept

A video news release (VNR) is just like a television news story. It must be objective as well as sound and look like a news report. Since television news stories run between one minute and 90 seconds each, your VNR should fall within that time frame. Package it in a format that's ready for on-the-air use but also allows stations to edit the material. The bottom line with VNRs, as with any other publicity material, is that you have to think like a journalist. If you can do that, the airplay you get for your VNR can be worth hundreds of thousands of dollars.

Producing a VNR is a complex process. Your first step is to produce a concept for it. A good concept will help you get organized, stay on track, and work effectively with your video production house. Use this worksheet to develop your concept. Depending on your time frame and the producer's preference, you may want to produce storyboards, with sketches, dialogue, and shooting directions for each scene.

The goal of this VNR is _____

_____

There are two helpful formulas for developing VNRs, although you can develop your own. Try them both to see which one works best for each VNR you produce.

## Formula 1

1. Identify a problem; this becomes your news peg.

_____

_____

2. Explain how your product, service, or organization solves the problem.

_____

_____

3. Summarize the problem and the solution.

_____

_____

_____

_____

## Formula 2

1. A reporter puts the story in perspective.

_____

# Creating the Video Concept

_____

_____

2. Sound bite 1 is 10 to 20 seconds using the voice of newsmaker one.

_____

_____

3. A narrator puts sound bite 1 in perspective and makes the transition to the next sound bite.

_____

4. Sound bite 2 is 10 to 20 seconds using the voice of newsmaker two.

_____

_____

5. The narrator puts sound bite 2 in perspective and makes the transition to the next sound bite.

_____

6. Sound bite 3 is 10 to 20 seconds using the voice of newsmaker three.

_____

_____

7. The reporter draws a brief conclusion and closes the story.

_____

You can get more mileage out of your video shoot if you use it for more than one purpose. Can you use this shoot to produce several VNRs with different news pegs or short features on related topics for television placement? Write your ideas below, and then work with your producer to make sure you get all the shots you'll need.

News peg for primary VNR:

_____

Video news releases with different news pegs:

1. _____

2. _____

3. _____

# Creating the Video Concept

Short features:

1. _____

2. _____

3. _____

You might want to make several versions of your VNR with narration in other languages for placement on American foreign-language television or abroad.

☐ English      ☐ Spanish      ☐ French      ☐ Mandarin Chinese
☐ Other _____      ☐ Other _____      ☐ Other _____

If you want a product mention in your VNR, you have to work your product into the story, so it seems like a natural part of it, and the story will fall apart without it. Write down your ideas for achieving this.

1. _____

2. _____

3. _____

4. _____

5. _____

What are the most important *facts* you want to present in this VNR?

1. _____

2. _____

3. _____

4. _____

5. _____

What are the most important *opinions* you want to present in this VNR? Limit the number of opinions so your VNR has a definite focus, and be sure to have the opinions expressed by the newsmakers, not by the narrator or reporter.

1. _____

2. _____

3. _____

List your spokespeople (newsmakers) below and indicate whether they need a tightly written script or general instructions.

# Creating the Video Concept

1. _____ Needs: _____

2. _____ Needs: _____

3. _____ Needs: _____

Local-angle VNRs get better placement. You can localize a VNR by adding local material to the "B-roll," the extra material you include that journalists can use to produce their own story or turn your short story into an in-depth version. Always mention local-angle material in the pitch letter that goes with your VNR. Write your local angle ideas below.

_____

_____

_____

Local experts from your organization, affiliated organizations, distributors, and dealers can add a local perspective. You can arrange to have them interviewed and include this material in the B-roll, or you can ask the television stations to do the interviewing. List them below.

Name: _____ Expertise: _____

Phone number: _____

Has agreed  ☐ Yes  ☐ No

Remarks: _____

Name: _____ Expertise: _____

Phone number: _____

Has agreed  ☐ Yes  ☐ No

Remarks: _____

Name: _____ Expertise: _____

Phone number: _____

Has agreed  ☐ Yes  ☐ No

Remarks: _____

Name: _____ Expertise: _____

Phone number: _____

Has agreed  ☐ Yes  ☐ No

Remarks: _____

# Creating the Video Concept

Statistics, facts, and figures from each local area can add a local angle to your VNR. Write down your ideas for this localized material below.

1. _____

2. _____

3. _____

4. _____

Plan each shot for your VNR in the next section. Whenever possible, shoot on location; this makes your VNR more interesting visually. If you have to shoot in a studio, use props, stage settings, and backdrops to make the set look as realistic as possible.

1. A reporter puts the story in perspective.

Reporter's name: _____

☐ Location Shot: _____

    ☐ Permit secured

    ☐ Reservation made

    ☐ Producer has scouted location

    ☐ Lighting needed: _____

    ☐ Crowd control needed: _____

    ☐ Props needed: _____

    ☐ Props secured

☐ Studio shot:

    ☐ Props needed: _____

    ☐ Props secured

    ☐ Backdrop needed: _____

    ☐ Backdrop secured

    ☐ Stage setting needed: _____

    ☐ Stage setting secured

Write dialogue here: _____

_____

# Creating the Video Concept

Dialogue time: _____ seconds

2. Sound bite 1 is 10 to 20 seconds using the voice of newsmaker one.

Newsmaker one's name: _____

☐ Location Shot: _____

    ☐ Permit secured

    ☐ Reservation made

    ☐ Producer has scouted location

    ☐ Lighting needed: _____

    ☐ Crowd control needed: _____

    ☐ Props needed: _____

    ☐ Props secured

☐ Studio shot:

    ☐ Props needed: _____

    ☐ Props secured

    ☐ Backdrop needed: _____

    ☐ Backdrop secured

    ☐ Stage setting needed: _____

    ☐ Stage setting secured

☐ Types of shots and how they will be used:

    ☐ Establishing: _____

    ☐ Zoom in: _____

    ☐ Static: _____

    ☐ Cover footage: _____

    ☐ Zoom out: _____

# Creating the Video Concept

Write dialogue here: _____

_____

_____

Dialogue time: _____ seconds

3. A narrator puts sound bite 1 in perspective and makes the transition to the next sound bite.

4. Sound bite 2 is 10 to 20 seconds using the voice of newsmaker two.

Newsmaker two's name: _____

☐ Location shot: _____

    ☐ Permit secured

    ☐ Reservation made

    ☐ Producer has scouted location

    ☐ Lighting needed: _____

    ☐ Crowd control needed: _____

    ☐ Props needed: _____

    ☐ Props secured

☐ Studio shot:

    ☐ Props needed: _____

    ☐ Props secured

    ☐ Backdrop needed: _____

    ☐ Backdrop secured

    ☐ Stage setting needed: _____

    ☐ Stage setting secured

☐ Types of shots and how they will be used:

    ☐ Establishing: _____

    ☐ Zoom in: _____

# Creating the Video Concept

☐ Static: _____

☐ Cover footage: _____

☐ Zoom out: _____

Write dialogue here: _____

_____

_____

Dialogue time: _____ seconds

5.  The narrator puts sound bite 2 in perspective and makes the transition to the next sound bite.

6.  Sound bite 3 is 10 to 20 seconds using the voice of newsmaker three.

Newsmaker three's name: _____

☐ Location Shot: _____

   ☐ Permit secured

   ☐ Reservation made

   ☐ Producer has scouted location

   ☐ Lighting needed: _____

   ☐ Crowd control needed: _____

   ☐ Props needed: _____

   ☐ Props secured

☐ Studio shot:

   ☐ Props needed: _____

   ☐ Props secured

   ☐ Backdrop needed: _____

   ☐ Backdrop secured

   ☐ Stage setting needed: _____

   ☐ Stage setting secured

# Creating the Video Concept

☐ Types of shots and how they will be used:

    ☐ Establishing: _____

    ☐ Zoom in: _____

    ☐ Static: _____

    ☐ Cover footage: _____

    ☐ Zoom out: _____

Write dialogue here: _____

_____

_____

Dialogue time: _____ seconds

7. Reporter draws a brief conclusion, closes story.
   Reporter's name: _____

☐ Location shot: _____

    ☐ Permit secured

    ☐ Reservation made

    ☐ Producer has scouted location

    ☐ Lighting needed: _____

    ☐ Crowd control needed: _____

    ☐ Props needed: _____

    ☐ Props secured

☐ Studio shot:

    ☐ Props needed: _____

    ☐ Props secured

    ☐ Backdrop needed: _____

    ☐ Backdrop secured

    ☐ Stage setting needed: _____

# Creating the Video Concept

☐ Stage setting secured

Write dialogue here: _____

_____

_____

Dialogue time: _____ seconds

A good "B-roll" can increase airplay for your VNR. List below what types of material you will include in your B-roll:

☐ Foreign language narration: _____

☐ Localized material (see previous section)

☐ A longer version of the edited story, with these additions:

_____

_____

_____

_____

☐ Extra sound bites:

_____

_____

_____

_____

☐ Extra establishing shots:

_____

_____

☐ Extra zoom-in shots:

_____

_____

# Creating the Video Concept

☐ Extra zoom-out shots:

_____

_____

☐ Coverage footage:

_____

_____

For related worksheets, see:

Checklist #13: Video Production Approvals
Checklist #14: Selecting Newsworthy Facts
Checklist #15: Developing a News Peg or Angle
Checklist #19: Increasing Publicity Placements With Local Angles
Checklist #21: Writing and Editing News Releases
Checklist #36: Preparing News Releases for Broadcasters
Checklist #37: Technical Requirements for Video News Releases
Checklist #38: Pitching Video News Releases
Checklist #54: The Right Production House for Your Video News Release

# 25

# Invitations to Press Conferences and Special Events

Invitations for press conferences and special events are similar. They should always be typed with wide margins and limited to one page. Include your organization's name and contact person's name, address, and telephone number at the top of the sheet. Use a format that covers who, when, where, why, how, and what. Above all else, prove that this event will be a news-maker by including hard facts. Mention any photographic possibilities. If the conference or event is not in a well-known location, include travel directions. Use this worksheet to create your media event invitations.

Date: _____

Product/service: _____

Project: _____

Topic: _____

Purpose: _____

Date: _____ Day:_____ Time _____

Location: _____ Site at Location: _____

Travel directions: _____

Speakers (from Checklist #12):

Name: _____

Qualifications and background: _____

_____

Name: _____

Qualifications and background: _____

_____

Name: _____

Qualifications and background: _____

_____

☐  Television-quality lighting available

☐  Broadcast-quality sound system on site

# Invitations to Press Conferences

Photo opportunities:

Subject: _____ Time: _____

Subject: _____ Time: _____

Subject: _____ Time: _____

Subject: _____ Time: _____

Brief background statement of 50 words or less (from Worksheet #12):

_____

_____

_____

_____

_____

For related worksheets, see:

Checklist #12: Planning Press Conferences and Special Events
Checklist #15: Developing a News Peg or Angle
Checklist #16: Formats for Printed Publicity Material
Checklist #48: Getting Photographic Coverage

# 26

# Planning Satellite Media Tours

Not long ago, the only way for a spokesperson to appear on local television talk and news shows across the United States was to physically travel to the studios in each target city. That was expensive for the organization, and time consuming and exhausting for the spokesperson. Today, a satellite media tour (SMT) lets the spokesperson travel to a single television studio. The tour operator prearranges as many as 25 interviews a day with talk show producers and news directors at television stations all over the country. The studio feeds a broadcast signal to a communications satellite, and, one after another, the television stations use their satellite dishes to capture that signal. The stations can see and hear your spokesperson, who will appear to be live on camera as far as their viewers are concerned. And your spokesperson can hear the interviewer, even though she can't actually see him or her. Use this checklist to develop a successful SMT.

Date: _____

Product/Service: _____

Project: _____

1. What is the goal of this tour?

   _____

2. Who is the spokesperson?

   _____

   Is a contract needed?　☐ Yes　☐ No　☐ Signed

3. Does he or she need training (see Checklist #39)?

   ☐ Yes　☐ No

4. How much lead time does your SMT operator need for tours that don't involve breaking news?

   _____ weeks

5. Can you stage it on location, rather than in a studio, so it's more visually interesting?

   ☐ Can shoot on site

   ☐ Must shoot in a studio. Explain: _____

   _____

6. For on-site SMTs, have the following been checked?

   ☐ Permit secured

# Planning Satellite Media Tours

- ☐ Reservation made

- ☐ Producer has scouted location

- ☐ Lighting needed:_____

- ☐ Crowd control needed: _____

- ☐ Props needed: _____

- ☐ Props secured

7. For studio SMTs, have the following been checked?

- ☐ Props needed: _____

- ☐ Props secured

- ☐ Backdrop needed: _____

- ☐ Backdrop secured

- ☐ Stage setting needed: _____

- ☐ Stage setting secured

8. Have you selected stations to offer your tour on an exclusive basis in each metropolitan area? If not, you must let each station know that your SMT is not an exclusive.

9. Have you checked to make sure there is either a teleprompter or cue card for each station on the tour? Your spokesperson must remember which city he or she is "in" and which station he or she is "on." Without these devices, it's easy to become confused and stumble, which could be embarrassing.

10. Has your spokesperson practiced looking straight at the camera while talking? While not important for a regular TV appearance, this is critical for an SMT, where the spokesperson cannot see the host or hostess.

11. Have you arranged for the tour coordinator to introduce your spokesperson to each interviewer before the actual interview starts? Allowing time for a bit of relaxed banter can set the right tone and help make the entire interview better.

For related worksheets, see:
Checklist #39: Live Appearance Checklist
Checklist #55: The Right Production House for Your Satellite Media Tour

# 27 Recycling Your Publicity

Your publicity can often be used again to get further publicity and to promote your organization and your product line. Reprints of newspaper or magazine articles give your organization and product line tremendous credibility, and tapes of radio or television coverage can be better than anything you produce in-house. You can also reprint an article in booklet form or duplicate a tape, offer one of them free to the public, publicize that offer, and get still more publicity in the process. Make sure your release has enough information to be interesting, but not so much that the audience will not have an incentive to send for the free booklet or tape.

Sometimes these recycling projects will involve other departments. When you approach the sales or marketing departments, be aware that you are bringing gifts that can gain you powerful allies. But also keep in mind that some people may be threatened by materials they didn't create themselves. You may have to allay their fears before they will use your materials, no matter how good the information is.

Date: _____

Product/Service: _____

Project: _____

Is the coveage completely positive?

☐ Yes (Recycle it)

☐ No (Don't recycle it)

Is there anything about this material that bothers you or that you don't think is perfect?

☐ Yes (Don't recycle it)

☐ No (Recycle it)

What objectives does the material meet? Fill them in below:

1. _____

2. _____

3. _____

☐ These objectives are important to us. (Recycle it)

☐ These objectives are *not* important to us. (Don't recycle it)

☐ Rate the strength of the material on a scale of 1 to 10, with 10 being the strongest. If the score is 8 or better, recycle it; if the rank is 7 or lower, don't.

# Recycling Your Publicity

Rank: _____

I have contacted the publication that ran the article or the broadcaster who aired the material about copyright status. We have agreed to the following:

☐ We own the copyright, and we are free to recycle the material

    ☐ with a credit to them.

    ☐ without a credit to them.

☐ They own the copyright, but we are free to recycle the material

    ☐ with a credit to them.

    ☐ without a credit to them.

☐ They own the copyright, and they do not want us to recycle the material.

☐ A copy of their letter or a memo summarizing my conversation, including the names of people I talked to is

    ☐ attached to this worksheet.

    ☐ filed in _____ .

The best use for this material is the following:

☐ Republicized as a free booklet or tape. Why? _____

☐ Turn over to the sales department for use as sales support material.
Why? _____

☐ Turn over to the marketing department for use in promotions and direct-mail campaigns.
Why? _____

Interdepartmental Contact Record

Contacted _____ in the _____ department on _____
            (name)                                            (date)

Results: _____

Contacted _____ in the _____ department on _____
            (name)                                            (date)

Results: _____

Contacted _____ in the _____ department on _____
            (name)                                            (date)

Results: _____

# Recycling Your Publicity

Contacted _____ in the _____ department on _____
                  (name)                                                                        (date)

Results: _____

For related worksheets, see:

Checklist #15: Developing a News Peg or Angle

# Part IV

# Newspaper and Magazine Publicity Materials

Journalists at newspapers and magazines have different requirements than broadcast journalists have. The checklists in this section will help you gather information about the needs and policies of the specific print media you work with, and organize that data in a format that will help you approach print journalists effectively.

You will also find step-by-step checklists that help you plan, conceptualize, shoot, process and submit top notch publicity photos that appeal to journalists, whether you have a staff photographer or you hire freelancers.

# 28 | Newspaper Policies and Specialized Reporters

The better you understand the policies and procedures, as well as which reporters handle specialized stories at each of the newspapers you approach for publicity, the more fruitful your results will be. Use this worksheet to gather this information for each newspaper on your publicity distribution list.

Date: _____

Name of newspaper: _____

Does this newspaper have a written policy on the types of stories it will run?

☐ Yes   ☐ No

Have you called the city editor or the community affairs office to see if you can get a copy?

☐ Yes   ☐ No

If you can't get a copy, are there other publicists who can give you background information on this paper's policies and procedures?

☐ Yes   ☐ No

Publicist's name: _____ Phone: _____

Date called: _____ Information received: _____

_____

_____

Publicist's name: _____ Phone: _____

Date called: _____ Information received: _____

_____

_____

Publicist's name: _____ Phone: _____

Date called: _____ Information received: _____

_____

_____

Does this newspaper have local news bureaus?

☐ Yes   ☐ No

# Newspaper Policies/Reporters

How do they want you to contact them?

☐ Headquarters only

☐ News bureaus only

☐ Depends on situation. Guidelines for deciding:

_____

_____

_____

List all the specialized editors and reporters with whom you may want to work. Include their deadline times, so you can avoid calling them then, unless you have a major, breaking news story. Also list their preferences and interests.

Art       Name: _____ Phone: _____ Deadline times: _____

Remarks and preferences: _____

Name: _____ Phone: _____ Deadline times: _____

Remarks and preferences: _____

Books    Name: _____ Phone: _____ Deadline times: _____

Remarks and preferences: _____

Name: _____ Phone: _____ Deadline times: _____

Remarks and preferences: _____

Business   Name: _____ Phone: _____ Deadline times: _____

Remarks and preferences: _____

Name: _____ Phone: _____ Deadline times: _____

Remarks and preferences: _____

Name: _____ Phone: _____ Deadline times: _____

Remarks and preferences: _____

Name: _____ Phone: _____ Deadline times: _____

Remarks and preferences: _____

Computers   Name: _____ Phone: _____ Deadline times: _____

Remarks and preferences: _____

# Newspaper Policies/Reporters

**Dance**   Name: _____ Phone: _____ Deadline times: _____

Remarks and preferences: _____

**Editorial**   Name: _____ Phone: _____ Deadline times: _____

Remarks and preferences: _____

Name: _____ Phone: _____ Deadline times: _____

Remarks and preferences: _____

Name: _____ Phone: _____ Deadline times: _____

Remarks and preferences: _____

Name: _____ Phone: _____ Deadline times: _____

Remarks and preferences: _____

**Education**   Name: _____ Phone: _____ Deadline times: _____

Remarks and preferences: _____

Name: _____ Phone: _____ Deadline times: _____

Remarks and preferences: _____

**Entertainment** Name: _____ Phone: _____ Deadline times: _____

Remarks and preferences: _____

Name: _____ Phone: _____ Deadline times: _____

Remarks and preferences: _____

**Events Calendar**   Name: _____ Phone: _____ Deadline times: _____

Remarks and preferences: _____

Name: _____ Phone: _____ Deadline times: _____

Remarks and preferences: _____

**Family Pages**   Name: _____ Phone: _____ Deadline times: _____

Remarks and preferences: _____

Name: _____ Phone: _____ Deadline times: _____

Remarks and preferences: _____

# Newspaper Policies/Reporters

Fashion    Name: _____ Phone: _____ Deadline times: _____

Remarks and preferences: _____

Name: _____ Phone: _____ Deadline times: _____

Remarks and preferences: _____

Features    Name: _____ Phone: _____ Deadline times: _____

Remarks and preferences: _____

Name: _____ Phone: _____ Deadline times: _____

Remarks and preferences: _____

Name: _____ Phone: _____ Deadline times: _____

Remarks and preferences: _____

Name: _____ Phone: _____ Deadline times: _____

Remarks and preferences: _____

Food    Name: _____ Phone: _____ Deadline times: _____

Remarks and preferences: _____

Name: _____ Phone: _____ Deadline times: _____

Remarks and preferences: _____

Foreign Affairs    Name: _____ Phone: _____ Deadline times: _____

Remarks and preferences: _____

Name: _____ Phone: _____ Deadline times: _____

Remarks and preferences: _____

Home and Garden    Name: _____ Phone: _____ Deadline times: _____

Remarks and preferences: _____

Name: _____ Phone: _____ Deadline times: _____

Remarks and preferences: _____

Movies    Name: _____ Phone: _____ Deadline times: _____

Remarks and preferences: _____

Name: _____ Phone: _____ Deadline times: _____

Remarks and preferences: _____

# Newspaper Policies/Reporters

Music      Name: _____ Phone: _____ Deadline times: _____

Remarks and preferences: _____

Name: _____ Phone: _____ Deadline times: _____

Remarks and preferences: _____

News      Name: _____ Phone: _____ Deadline times: _____

Remarks and preferences: _____

Name: _____ Phone: _____ Deadline times: _____

Remarks and preferences: _____

Name: _____ Phone: _____ Deadline times: _____

Remarks and preferences: _____

Name: _____ Phone: _____ Deadline times: _____

Remarks and preferences: _____

Real Estate    Name: _____ Phone: _____ Deadline times: _____

Remarks and preferences: _____

Name: _____ Phone: _____ Deadline times: _____

Remarks and preferences: _____

Science     Name: _____ Phone: _____ Deadline times: _____

Remarks and preferences: _____

Name: _____ Phone: _____ Deadline times: _____

Remarks and preferences: _____

Society     Name: _____ Phone: _____ Deadline times: _____

Remarks and preferences: _____

Name: _____ Phone: _____ Deadline times: _____

Remarks and preferences: _____

Sports      Name: _____ Phone: _____ Deadline times: _____

Remarks and preferences: _____

Name: _____ Phone: _____ Deadline times: _____

Remarks and preferences: _____

# Newspaper Policies/Reporters

Suburban Affairs   Name: _____ Phone: _____ Deadline times: _____

Remarks and preferences: _____

Name: _____ Phone: _____ Deadline times: _____

Remarks and preferences: _____

Sunday Editors   Name: _____ Phone: _____ Deadline times: _____

Remarks and preferences: _____

Name: _____ Phone: _____ Deadline times: _____

Remarks and preferences: _____

Television   Name: _____ Phone: _____ Deadline times: _____

Remarks and preferences: _____

Name: _____ Phone: _____ Deadline times: _____

Remarks and preferences: _____

Theater   Name: _____ Phone: _____ Deadline times: _____

Remarks and preferences: _____

Name: _____ Phone: _____ Deadline times: _____

Remarks and preferences: _____

Travel   Name: _____ Phone: _____ Deadline times: _____

Remarks and preferences: _____

Name: _____ Phone: _____ Deadline times: _____

Remarks and preferences: _____

Other _____

Name: _____ Phone: _____ Deadline times: _____

Remarks and preferences: _____

Name: _____ Phone: _____ Deadline times: _____

Remarks and preferences: _____

Other _____

Name: _____ Phone: _____ Deadline times: _____

Remarks and preferences: _____

# Newspaper Policies/Reporters

For related worksheets, see:

Checklist #41: Broadcasters' Policies for Public Service Announcements
Checklist #43: Journalist Contact Preferences
Checklist #44: Telephone Contact Strategy Worksheet
Checklist #45: Telephoning Broadcast Journalists
Checklist #46: Contacting News Bureaus

# Pitching Feature Stories to Newspapers and Magazines

Feature stories are usually not based on hard, breaking news. They often have a human interest aspect, and they are usually longer than news stories. At larger publications, the staff will get information from you and other sources and do the writing themselves. Journalists at smaller publications, on the other hand, may welcome finished feature stories. Whether you supply information or write them yourself, feature stories can give you incredibly useful coverage. It's worth planning them carefully, starting with your approach to the journalists involved, which can be by telephone or in writing.

Keep in mind that feature stories are almost always exclusive. Journalists will be very angry if their competition runs feature material they thought was their exclusive, and competition includes radio and television. If you're placing feature stories in local publications, you can usually arrange exclusivity on a geographical basis, so you can place a story in many local newspapers that don't overlap. But always ask journalists first!

Use this worksheet to plan your pitch for a feature story.

Date: _____

Product/service: _____

Project: _____

I am going to make my pitch

☐ by telephone.

☐ in writing.

Before I make my pitch, I have determined that:

☐ This magazine uses outside writers, so I should offer to supply a completed article.

☐ This magazine never uses outside writers, so I should *not* offer to supply a completed article.

☐ I am pitching this story to a national publication, so I can't pitch it to anyone else.

☐ I am pitching this story to a single publication in my local area.

My first choice is _____

My second choice is _____

My third choice is _____

☐ I am pitching this story to publications in more than one local area.

　　☐ I have checked to see that their circulations do not overlap.

　　☐ I have informed the journalists involved.

# Pitching Feature Stories

☐ I have looked at the editorial calendars of these magazines to see where my feature story ideas might fit in.

☐ I have looked at the guidelines for writers from these magazines to see what they're looking for.

I have the following *information* ready to make my pitch:

1. _____

2. _____

3. _____

4. _____

5. _____

6. _____

7. _____

8. _____

I have the following *facts and figures* ready to make my pitch:

1. _____

2. _____

3. _____

4. _____

5. _____

6. _____

7. _____

8. _____

I have the following *anecdotes* ready to make my pitch:

1. _____

2. _____

3. _____

4. _____

# Pitching Feature Stories

5. _____

6. _____

7. _____

8. _____

I have the following *photos*, *illustrations* or *suggestions* ready to make my pitch:

1. _____

2. _____

3. _____

4. _____

5. _____

6. _____

7. _____

8. _____

Prepare your feature pitch carefully, whether you plan to make it by telephone or in writing. Use the following outline.

1. Tell the editor you are offering a feature story.

2. Summarize the idea in one 20- to 30-word paragraph.

_____

_____

_____

_____

3. Explain why the editor's audience would be interested (what's in it for them), in one 20- to 30-word paragraph.

_____

_____

_____

# Pitching Feature Stories

4. Discuss the scope of the story—what it will cover and why it is important. Limit yourself to two 20- to 30-word paragraphs.

_____

_____

_____

_____

_____

_____

5. Give a few fascinating facts or interesting anecdotes from your previous list. Limit yourself to one 20- to 30-word paragraph.

_____

_____

_____

_____

6. Suggest alternate news pegs.

1. _____

2. _____

3. _____

7. Describe possibilities for photos or illustrations. Limit yourself to two 15- to 20-word paragraphs:

_____

_____

_____

_____

_____

8. Offer to supply either raw material or a complete, finished story, depending on the journalist's preference.

# Pitching Feature Stories

9. Enclose a prepaid post card with a toll-free number, or an offer to accept collect calls if the editor is interested in discussing your feature story further.

Before I start work on producing a complete article, I have reached a clear understanding with the editor about the following:

☐ How long the article should be: _____

☐ The editor's format preferences

    ☐ manuscript

    ☐ 5.25" computer disk

    ☐ 3.5" computer disk

        ☐ using _____ word processing program

        ☐ ASCII

☐ The editor's approval of a detailed outline

☐ The editor's tentative publication date: _____

I need the following approvals from people in my organization before I can submit this article.

1. Legal department _____

2. _____

3. _____

4. _____

## Production Schedule

Work backward, with the last date first. Items marked with an asterisk should be agreed to by the editor.

_____ Due at magazine*

_____ Ready to deliver by ☐ overnight courier

                               ☐ express mail

                               ☐ other _____

_____ Rewritten

_____ Approvals from people in my organization requested

_____ Approvals from people in my organization received

_____ Photos ready

# Pitching Feature Stories

_____  Edited and proofread

_____  Photo proof sheets examined; shots chosen

_____  Rewritten

_____  Distancing time (let it sit so you have perspective when you rewrite)

_____  Photos shot

_____  First draft

_____  Outline approved by editor*

_____  Outline to editor by*   ☐ overnight courier

                                          ☐ express mail

                                          ☐ other _____

_____  Outline completed

_____  Research completed

For related worksheets, see:

Checklist #14: Selecting Newsworthy Facts
Checklist #15: Developing a News Peg or Angle
Checklist #22: Working with Writers

# 30

# Writing Letters to the Editor

The "Letters to the Editor" section is one of the most widely read sections of the newspaper, which makes it a great place to get publicity. Letters to the editor are most useful to correct inaccurate information that appeared in the publication or to address a controversial issue of importance to your organization or industry. You can sometimes get your product mentioned in a letter to the editor of a specialized section of the newspaper or a specialized publication.

Follow the steps in this section to write a powerful letter to the editor about an issue or controversy.

1. Choose *just one* issue for your letter:

   _____

2. Write a 15- to 20-word paragraph that identifies your organization and states the purpose of your letter.

   _____

   _____

   _____

3. Write one or two 15- to 20-word paragraphs that give background material on the issue. Do not include opinions here, save them for later.

   _____

   _____

   _____

   _____

   _____

4. Give your opinion(s) in one 15- to 20-word paragraph.

   _____

   _____

   _____

5. State a solution and ask the reader to take a concrete action, like calling or writing a government official. Limit this section to one 15- to 20-word paragraph.

   _____

   _____

6. Assemble the parts, type the letter, address it "Dear Editor," proofread it, and mail it.

Follow the steps in this section to write a powerful letter to the editor about a misconception.

1. Choose *just one* misconception for your letter:

_____

2. Write a 10- to 15-word paragraph that briefly mentions the misconception but does not dwell on it. The focus should be on correct information in item 3.

_____

_____

_____

3. Write one or two 15- to 20-word paragraphs that give solid evidence countering the misconception. Cite impartial, third-party sources whenever possible.

_____

_____

_____

_____

_____

4. Write one 20- to 25-word paragraph that asks the editor to inform his or her readers about the evidence, and summarize the evidence in five to ten words.

_____

_____

_____

_____

5. Assemble the parts, type the letter, address it "Dear Editor," proofread it, and mail it.

For related worksheets, see:

Checklist #5: Using Misconceptions to Your Advantage

# 31

# Evaluating Magazines as Publicity Outlets

Magazines can be very fruitful publicity outlets, if you understand how to choose the right publication for your story. There's no shortcut here—you'll have to read and evaluate several issues of each magazine you want to target. Use this worksheet to build a "publicist's portrait" of each magazine you evaluate.

Title of Magazine: _____

Type of magazine:

☐ General interest consumer          ☐ Special interest consumer

☐ Business          ☐ Trade

Does this magazine have specialized reporters:

☐ Yes (fill in below)          ☐ No

| Name | Specialty | Telephone |
|------|-----------|-----------|
| _____ | _____ | _____ |
| _____ | _____ | _____ |
| _____ | _____ | _____ |
| _____ | _____ | _____ |
| _____ | _____ | _____ |
| _____ | _____ | _____ |
| _____ | _____ | _____ |

Does this magazine have local bureaus?

☐ Yes (fill in below)          ☐ No

| Bureau City | Address | Telephone | Specialized Reporters Name | Specialty |
|-------------|---------|-----------|------------------|-----------|
| _____ | _____ | _____ | _____ | _____ |
| | | | _____ | _____ |
| | | | _____ | _____ |

# Evaluating Magazines

| Bureau City | Address | Telephone | Specialized Reporters Name | Specialty |
|---|---|---|---|---|
| _____ | _____ | _____ | _____ | _____ |
| | | | _____ | _____ |
| | | | _____ | _____ |
| _____ | _____ | _____ | _____ | _____ |
| | | | _____ | _____ |
| | | | _____ | _____ |
| _____ | _____ | _____ | _____ | _____ |
| | | | _____ | _____ |
| | | | _____ | _____ |

How do they want you to contact them?

☐ Headquarters only.

☐ News bureaus only.

☐ Both. Guidelines for deciding: _____

_____

What regular features or columns do they have that interest you?

| Name | Types of Materials Used | Contact Name |
|---|---|---|
| _____ | _____ | _____ |
| _____ | _____ | _____ |
| _____ | _____ | _____ |
| _____ | _____ | _____ |

Does the magazine have an editorial calendar that lists topics of upcoming issues? This is an extremely useful tool that helps you plan ahead to meet the needs of journalists and increase the possibility you'll get coverage. Call the advertising department at the magazine and ask for a copy.

☐ I asked for a copy on _____ .

☐ They do not have an editorial calendar.

# Evaluating Magazines

Does the magazine have guidelines for writers? This document can help you understand what the editors are looking for and increase the chances of placing a feature article. Call the editorial department at the magazine and ask for a copy.

☐  I asked for a copy on _____ .

☐  They do not have guidelines for writers.

How often is this magazine published?

☐  Weekly        ☐  Every two weeks

☐  Twice a month     ☐  Monthly

☐  Other _____

I should avoid calling this magazine at the following deadline time, except about breaking hard news stories:

_____

This magazine needs _____ days/weeks/months of lead time.

Remarks and comments:

_____

_____

For related worksheets, see:

Checklist #29: Pitching Feature Stories to Newspapers and Magazines

# Hiring a News Photographer

# 32

A good news photographer can compose a powerful publicity photo on the spot and have finished photos in your hands within hours. Someone who does not have news photography experience, on the other hand, may take weak and unfocussed shots that don't do the job. If you're not sure how to find a good news photographer, call your local newspaper, ask for the darkroom, and ask the person who answers the phone. Keep in mind that the darkroom may be dark when you call, so offer to call back later if necessary. You can often get the names of top-notch news photographers this way. Use this checklist each time you are hiring a news photographer to make sure he or she understands the assignment and that you have the legal bases covered.

☐ I have a written contract with the freelance photographer that has been approved by the legal department and which specifies the following:

- This is work performed for hire.

- Our organization owns all rights to this work, including the negatives.

- The photographer will not solicit or accept payment from the magazine, newspaper, or wire service.

- The photographer is an independent contractor, not an employee.

- The photographer is not under any contractual obligations that conflict with this agreement.

- The photographer will not get a credit line.

☐ The photographer has signed a memo of understanding (MOU) that outlines the assignment, including the following:

- The date of the event

- The address of the event

- The location at the address

- Travel directions to the event

- Your objectives for these photos

 —What do you want to achieve?

 —What do you want to emphasize?

 —What do you want to de-emphasize?

- The due date and time for the shots

- The fee to be paid to the photographer

- Payment of one half of the photographer's fee on signing the MOU

- Whether the fee includes film, processing, and other expenses

- Limits on and documentation for expenses

- No payment beyond the first if the photos are unsatisfactory

# Hiring a News Photographer

- Payment of the second half of the photographer's fee within five days of delivery of the photos and the negatives, unless they are unsatisfactory

- The news peg for the story

For related worksheets, see:

Checklist #33: Technical Requirements for News Photos
Checklist #34: Shooting Newsworthy Photos of People and Events
Checklist #35: Product Photography

# 33

# Technical Requirements for News Photos

The publicity shot of the century probably won't get used if it doesn't meet the technical requirements of newspapers and magazines. Use the following checklist to make sure your news photos are technically good enough so editors will welcome them. Since product publicity photos have somewhat different technical requirements, see Checklist #35: Product Photography.

- Use a professional 35mm camera. If you're not sure that your camera is of professional quality, ask at your local camera shop.

- Send newspapers black-and-white glossies, unless you know for sure that they can use color shots.

- If you're working with newspapers that use color, find out on which pages the color runs and check with an editor to see if your story can run on one of those pages.

- Newspapers want photos that are at least 5" × 7" inches, or 4" × 5" for head shots (just a head and shoulders, not a full-body shot.)

- Photos lose contrast when they are reproduced on newsprint, so they must have strong contrast to begin with. Check each photo for strong contrast. If it doesn't have enough, don't send it out. If you really need that shot, ask your photo lab if they can reprint it with increased contrast.

- Most of your photos for newspapers should be vertical rather than horizontal, since vertical photos fit a newspaper format better.

- Magazines have a looser format. Ask magazine editors you work with if they prefer vertical or horizontal art.

- Your photos should have white margins around them, where the photo editor can indicate crop marks and other instructions.

- Avoid getting fingerprints on photos, writing on the back of photos, or using paper clips on them, which can make them impossible to reproduce.

- Include captions that tell the whole story, identify everyone in the shot, and have your organization's name, address, and telephone number, as well as the date. You should tape those to the backs of your photos.

- Make sure you have written, signed model releases from everyone appearing in your photos.

For related worksheets, see:

# 34

# Shooting Newsworthy Photos of People and Events

Journalists call good news pictures "art;" not museum-quality art, but artful communication. Yet publicity photos from businesses and nonprofit organizations are usually notoriously bad. There are simple techniques to make your publicity photos stand out from the usual awful pictures of people passing a check, breaking ground, and shaking hands. This checklist helps you take newsworthy publicity photos. See Checklist #48: Getting Photographic Coverage to find out how to get the media to accept your photos or provide photo coverage for you.

1. Plan your publicity photos ahead of time. What do you want them to accomplish? What message are you trying to convey to your audience? How will these photos convey that message?

2. Develop a news peg for your photos that is unusual and interesting.

3. If you are planning to use any of the following five standard clichés in publicity pictures, rethink your approach now. These cliches are:

   • One person passing a donation check to another

   • Someone breaking ground with a shovel

   • Two people shaking hands

   • Someone cutting a ribbon

   • One person passing an award plaque to another

   The problem with these themes is that they don't tell a story. If you don't know the people in the photo, it won't mean anything to you.

4. Make your photos of people show something about the relationship between them.

5. Show some action taking place whenever possible. Action shots make better art.

6. Show a product in action and include the users.

7. Show the benefit of a product.

8. Consider showing the benefit that will come from a donation rather than the ceremony celebrating the donation.

9. Capture the meaning of the ceremony to the participants, rather than the ceremony itself. You may need a "conceptual" shot here.

10. Consider using photo illustration to illustrate a concept. Conceptual shots are not easy, and you may need a professional photographer to develop them. But they make excellent art and dramatically improve your chances for publicity success.

11. Ask someone who knows nothing about your business or organization and the event shown in your photo to tell you what's going on without a caption. If they can't, the photo is not newsworthy.

12. Avoid "picket-fence" shots by grouping your subjects imaginatively, not in a straight, side-by-side line.

13. Keep your groups small—five people or fewer—unless you're using a professional photographer. It's very hard to photograph large groups well.

14. When you look at a photo, your eye should be immediately drawn to one place, called the point of interest. If you have more than one point of interest, your photos will be confusing and weak.

15. Whenever possible, include an object that identifies your organization in the shot.

16. Get a variety of vantage points by shifting your camera position. Most publicity art is shot head-on. Shoot from above, below, or from the side to get more interesting photos.

17. Use different lenses, f-stops, depth of field settings, and lighting arrangements to get shots with a wide range of effects.

18. Unless the shot is of patients in a clinic or a similar situation that demands confidentiality, all the people in the art should be identifiable.

19. Avoid backgrounds that detract from the important part of the picture. For example, don't take photos in front of windows or wallpaper with large, bright patterns.

20. Edit and crop the proofs before you have your final art printed. Use plain white pieces of paper to cover extraneous parts of the photo until you have the most powerful art possible. Then mark the proof with a red grease pencil, so the photo lab will know exactly how you want the finished art produced.

For related worksheets, see:

Checklist #32: Hiring a News Photograher
Checklist #33: Technical Requirements for News Photos
Checklist #35: Product Photography

# 35 Product Photography

The visual and technical approach for product publicity photos is quite different from publicity photos of people and events. Products have to look their best, and this often involves some complex manipulation of lighting and the product itself. Don't try to do product shots yourself. Hire a photographer with product shot experience. He or she will know how to make your product look its best and will have the right equipment to do it, including a large-format "view" camera that uses 4" × 5" or 8" × 10" film. The quality of your product shots is less important in newspapers, more important in magazines, and most important when the photograph will be enlarged. Use this checklist to plan your product shots with your photographer.

Date: _____

Product/service: _____

Project: _____

This shot will be sent to _____
(name of publication)

It wants:

☐ Color               ☐ Black and white

☐ People in the shots ☐ No people in the shots

☐ Photos              ☐ 4" × 5" transparencies    ☐ 8" × 10" transparencies

This shot will be sent to _____
(name of publication)

It wants:

☐ Color               ☐ Black and white

☐ People in the shots ☐ No people in the shots

☐ Photos              ☐ 4" × 5" transparencies    ☐ 8" × 10" transparencies

This shot will be sent to _____
(name of publication)

It wants:

☐ Color               ☐ Black and white

☐ People in the shots ☐ No people in the shots

☐ Photos              ☐ 4" × 5" transparencies    ☐ 8" × 10" transparencies

# Product Photography

This shot will be sent to _____
(name of publication)

It wants:

☐ Color                   ☐ Black and white

☐ People in the shots     ☐ No people in the shots

☐ Photos                  ☐ 4" × 5" transparencies     ☐ 8" × 10" transparencies

This shot will be sent to _____
(name of publication)

It wants:

☐ Color                   ☐ Black and white

☐ People in the shots     ☐ No people in the shots

☐ Photos                  ☐ 4" × 5" transparencies     ☐ 8" × 10" transparencies

This shot will be sent to _____
(name of publication)

It wants:

☐ Color                   ☐ Black and white

☐ People in the shots     ☐ No people in the shots

☐ Photos                  ☐ 4" × 5" transparencies     ☐ 8" × 10" transparencies

## Photo Shoot

The photo shoot will be on _____ at _____.

Travel directions: _____

_____

☐ The publicist will be at the shoot to approve each shot's set-up.

☐ The arrangement for set-up approvals is: _____

_____

Items needed that will be supplied by publicist:

1. _____

2. _____

3. _____

# Product Photography

4. _____

5. _____

6. _____

7. _____

8. _____

Items needed that will be supplied by photographer:

1. _____

2. _____

3. _____

4. _____

5. _____

6. _____

7. _____

8. _____

Will the photographer shoot test Polaroids®?

☐ Yes   ☐ No

## The Shots

Shot # _____ Description: _____

Background material: _____

People in photo?

☐ Yes. Doing what? _____

☐ No.

Props: _____

Other arrangements: _____

# Product Photography

Shot # _____ Description: _____

Background material: _____

People in photo?

☐ Yes. Doing what? _____

☐ No.

Props: _____

Other arrangements: _____

Shot # _____ Description: _____

Background material: _____

People in photo?

☐ Yes. Doing what? _____

☐ No.

Props: _____

Other arrangements: _____

Shot # _____ Description: _____

Background material: _____

People in photo?

☐ Yes. Doing what? _____

☐ No.

Props: _____

Other arrangements: _____

If you're shooting more than four photos, photocopy this sheet to enter information for the additional shots.

For related worksheets, see:

Checklist #32: Hiring a News Photographer
Checklist #33: Technical Requirements for News Photos
Checklist #34: Shooting Newsworthy Photos of People and Events

# Part V

# Radio and Television Publicity Materials

Conceptualizing, writing, and producing material designed to be heard and seen on the air involves meeting highly technical standards. Video news releases must be designed to meet television's journalistic and technical needs, the sound for radio public service announcements must be of "broadcast quality," and even a simple live appearance on the air involves scores of considerations.

The following checklists help you understand the two critical definitions of broadcast quality, and help you create, produce, and pitch video news releases, audio news releases, live appearances, and public service announcements designed to get the maximum possible coverage.

# 36 Preparing News Releases for Broadcasters

News releases designed for broadcast are different from releases designed for the print media. They must be shorter and designed to be spoken and heard, rather than read. Use this checklist to transform your print media news releases into broadcast material. It won't take you long to do and could increase your placement success.

1. Read your release out loud and time it. Since broadcast news programs often use very short stories, you should edit it down to between 20 and 30 seconds.

2. Read your news release out loud and cut out anything that's difficult to say.

3. Short sentences are important for broadcast material. Limit yours to 10 to 15 words each.

4. Avoid too many "s" sounds because they tend to hiss over the air.

5. Every time you use the words "she," "he," and "they," make it clear to whom they refer.

6. If you have homonyms that sound alike but have different meanings, make sure those meanings are clear from the context.

7. Type your broadcast news release, double-spaced, on 8½ × 11" white paper.

8. Leave wide margins at the top, bottom, and sides of the page to give the news director space to write instructions.

9. Include your organization's name and address, the date, the name and telephone number of a contact person, and the reading time in seconds in your heading.

10. Use the present tense and round out numbers.

11. Spell out phonetically any names that are difficult to pronounce. Do this after the name; for example, Yalowicsz (Yahl-oh-wits).

12. Keep background material to a minimum. If you consider supplementary information necessary, add a separate backgrounder sheet.

For related worksheets, see:

Checklist #21: Writing and Editing News Releases
Checklist #23: Meeting the Needs of Broadcast Journalists
Checklist #24: Creating the Video News Release Concept

# 37 Technical Requirements for Video News Releases

If you want broadcasters to run your video news release (VNR), it has to meet industry standards of broadcast quality. This term can be confusing, since it refers to both the technical format and the content. From a technical point of view, broadcast quality refers to measurable standards for the intensity of the signal on a tape. If the signal on the tape is too weak, it can't be broadcast and received clearly. That's why your VNR must be produced and edited by professionals using broadcast-quality equipment. But broadcast quality involves style as well as technical considerations. A VNR should look and sound like a local news story, not an advertisement or infomercial. Fancy visual effects, sound effects, and music are usually out of place in a VNR. Use this checklist to make sure your VNR meets industry technical standards.

1. Your VNR should be 90 seconds or less.

2. Shorten it even more by putting some of the material in a separate backgrounder, which you include in the extra material broadcasters call the "B-roll."

3. Always identify your organization as the source of the news.

4. Make sure your newsmakers speak in 10- to 20-second "sound bites."

5. Make sure your production house keeps the sound bites and narration on separate tracks.

6. Include two versions of the edited story: one with titles and one without.

7. Make sure your narrator never appears on screen. A TV station doesn't want nonstaff reporters appearing on its news show.

8. Your B-roll should include the following material which news editors can add to the basic story, or use to create their own:

   • Extra sound bites that elaborate on the story and go into more detail

   • Several alternate establishing shots that set the scene for the story

   • Extra static shots where the perspective is constant

   • Extra zoom-in and zoom-out shots where the camera moves into or back from the scene

   • Background material on the news story that goes into greater depth than the short, edited version

9. Include an index at the start of the tape, and enclose a printed copy with the support materials for the VNR.

10. The support package sent out to news directors should include a timed script, background material, and a pitch letter selling the VNR to news directors.

11. Make sure your production house has made both a dubbing master for duplicating copies and a second master for safekeeping.

# Video News Requirements

For related worksheets, see:

# 38 | Pitching Video News Releases

When you pitch a video news release (VNR) to a television news director, always consider how journalists feel about this news vehicle. News production budgets are being cut as broadcasters seek to fatten their bottom lines. But news shows are increasingly important profit generators, so they are being expanded. This means news directors are caught between the proverbial rock and a hard place. Journalists want to maintain their independence and write their own stories, but they don't always have the resources to do so. Instead of reminding them of this dilemma, present your VNR in a way that makes it so newsworthy they can't resist it. Whether you are pitching your VNR in writing, by telephone, or both, use this checklist to help you present it effectively.

1. Explain why the information is of interest and importance to the station's local viewers.

2. Discuss the news peg in 10 to 20 words.

3. Mention any well-known spokespeople who appear in this VNR.

4. Point out that this highly newsworthy material is not available from other sources.

5. Remind the news director that this material can't be easily produced locally.

6. Explain any local angle material or opportunities for adding local angles.

7. Describe the added material in the B-roll.

8. Point out that this VNR is of broadcast quality and will meet all the station's technical requirements.

9. If you're pitching by telephone, offer to send a timed script, background information on the newsmakers who appear in the VNR, and a written index for both tracks of the cassette. If you're making the pitch in writing, mention in your letter that you're including them.

10. If you're sending this pitch ahead of the actual videocassette with the VNR on it, be sure to include all the supporting material again in the package with the videocassette.

For related worksheets, see:

Checklist #24: Creating the Video News Release Concept
Checklist #37: Technical Requirements for Video News Releases

# 39

# Live Appearance Checklist

Live appearances on talk shows can be highly valuable publicity tools. Contact the talent booker for a talk show well in advance of the air date and explain why your spokesperson will be of interest to the station's audience, and how he or she fits in to the show's format. Follow up with a tip sheet, much like a press conference invitation. Then use this Checklist to prepare your spokesperson for media success.

Date: _____

Topic: _____

☐ Appearance on single show

☐ Appearances on multiple shows

| Date | Time | Show | Date | Time | Show |
|------|------|------|------|------|------|
| _____ | _____ | _____ | _____ | _____ | _____ |
| _____ | _____ | _____ | _____ | _____ | _____ |
| _____ | _____ | _____ | _____ | _____ | _____ |

Spokesperson: _____

Objective: _____

Anecdotes, examples, figures, and facts your speaker can use to make the story come alive:

_____

_____

_____

_____

_____

Key points you want your spokesperson to cover in an interview:

_____

_____

_____

_____

_____

# Live Appearance Checklist

How do you know how good this speaker is?_____

_____

Has your speaker practiced giving short, 10- to 15-second answers to interview questions on these topics?

☐ Yes   ☐ No

Does your spokesperson speak too fast or too slowly?

☐ Too fast   ☐ Too slowly   ☐ Just right

Does your talk show host or hostess want written questions submitted in advance? Do you know what format they're needed in?

☐ Yes (fill in below)   ☐ No

1. _____

2. _____

3. _____

4. _____

5. _____

6. _____

7. _____

8. _____

9. _____

10. _____

11. _____

12. _____

13. _____

14. _____

15. _____

16. _____

# Live Appearance Checklist

Is the spokesperson likely to encounter hostile, aggressive or rapid-fire questions?

☐ Yes. Practice sessions will be needed to formulate answers to anticipated questions and develop poise.

☐ No, because _____ .

Does the spokesperson have a monotone voice?

☐ Yes. Practice sessions will be needed to get him or her to vary tone.

☐ No.

Speaker's other rough spots that can be polished with practice:

_____

_____

_____

If you want a product credit on the show, have you discussed this with the station in advance?

☐ Yes   ☐ No

Does your speaker know how to dress for television success?

☐ Yes   ☐ No (go over the following material)

• Wear medium tones.

• Avoid clothing with stripes and bold checks.

• Choose an ivory, ecru, or pastel shirt or blouse instead of white, which glares.

* All jewelry must be non-reflective.

If your spokesperson has not appeared on the air before, have you briefed him or her about each of the following?

☐ Hand signals from the studio crew

☐ The range of any fixed microphones and how to position himself or herself

☐ Assuming all mikes are live

☐ Toning down gestures and moving more slowly than usual

☐ Looking at the interviewer unless he or she wants to address the audience directly

# Live Appearance Checklist

☐ Getting comfortable with the earphone used on a satellite media tour before the tour starts

☐ How to use teleprompters

For related worksheets, see:

Checklist #26: Planning Satellite Media Tours

# 40

# Public Service Announcements

Public service announcements (PSAs) are one of the most common kinds of publicity. Since they are short, broadcasters run a lot of them, and they are relatively easy to get. Many publicists believe that PSAs are available only to nonprofit organizations, but that's not true. If you take the "service" approach and provide material that will benefit your audience, and it is regarded as serving community interests, you have a good chance of your PSAs being used. They can be submitted in written format, to be read by the station's announcer, or prerecorded on an audiotape. Use this checklist to help you plan your PSAs so they are in the proper format.

1. Always give public service directors a choice of two or three lengths for your PSA.

2. You'll get more airplay if your PSAs do not mention fund-raising directly, even if you are working for a nonprofit organization.

3. Keep in mind that your audience will probably be doing something else besides just listening to and watching your PSA. You need to do something that will grab their interest immediately—and keep it.

4. Limit your PSA to one main point for maximum impact.

5. Close your PSA by asking people to take an action whenever possible.

6. Always be sure you can back up the facts, figures, and claims in your PSA. It's a good idea to file the back-up material with a copy of the PSA.

7. When you edit a PSA, cut out extra words, particularly adjectives.

8. Make sure prerecorded PSAs are exactly 10, 15, 20, 30, or 60 seconds long.

9. Make sure there is no sound in the first and last half-second on a prerecorded PSA.

10. For live-television PSAs, make sure you have one slide for each five to ten seconds and that the slides are all horizontal.

11. The script for a live-television PSA should describe each slide. Slides should be numbered and keyed to the script.

12. Plan to use professional recording studios with broadcast-quality equipment for PSAs. Home tape recorders and camcorders aren't good enough for producing broadcast-quality materials like PSAs.

13. Make sure you have permission to use the music and sound effects in prerecorded PSAs. Write it into your contract with the recording studio.

14. Always send a script or a storyboard with prerecorded spots.

15. Consider sending out a script and a prepaid request card, rather than massive numbers of

prerecorded PSAs. You'll get some airplay directly from the script, and those stations that do request cassettes will be more likely to use them.

16. Decide who will distribute your prerecorded PSAs.

17. Your PSA distributor must have an up-to-date station information database so they know which format each station prefers.

For related worksheets, see:

Checklist #41: Broadcasters' Policies for Public Service Announcements
Checklist #42: Getting Public Service Announcements for Businesses

# 41 Broadcasters' Policies for Public Service Announcements

Policies for public service announcements (PSAs) vary widely from one broadcaster to another. Make a copy of this worksheet for every broadcaster you want to work with, so you won't waste time and money pitching PSAs to stations that aren't interested.

Date this checklist was filled out: _____

Review this information again on: _____

Station name: _____ ☐ Radio ☐ TV

Address: _____

_____

Public service director's name: _____

Telephone number: _____

1. Have you asked if the station has a written policy about using PSAs?

☐ Yes, they don't have a policy.

☐ Yes, they promised to send a copy of the policy on _____ (date).

☐ Yes, a copy of their policy is filed _____ .

☐ No, but I will.

This station uses:

☐ live copy  ☐ prerecorded copy  ☐ both

☐ 10-second spots  ☐ 20-second spots  ☐ 30-second spots  ☐ 60-second spots

☐ glass-mounted slides only ☐ cardboard-mounted slides ☐ plastic-mounted slides

Other technical requirements:

_____

_____

# Broadcasters' Policies

Does the station require substantiation from nonprofit organizations?

Copies of fundraising permits from _____    ☐ Yes    ☐ No

Your IRS tax-status letter    ☐ Yes    ☐ No

For related worksheets, see:

Checklist #40: Public Service Announcements
Checklist #42: Getting Public Service Announcements for Businesses

# Getting Public Service Announcements for Businesses

Many publicists believe that PSAs are available only to nonprofit organizations, but that's not true. If you take the service approach and provide material that will benefit your audience, it is regarded as serving community interests, and there is a good chance your PSAs will be used. You can also sponsor PSAs for nonprofit organizations, which will then give you sponsor credit in the spot. With strategic planning, you can work in a product mention. But you must make it such an integral part of the PSA that it seems natural, not forced, and the PSA won't work without it. Use this worksheet to develop a plan for getting PSAs for your business.

- List five ways your business or trade association can present information in PSAs that serve community interests *and* meet your goals:

1. _____

2. _____

3. _____

4. _____

5. _____

- Run these ideas by several public service directors at broadcast stations to get their input. If it's positive, start creating your PSAs. If it's negative, see if they can help you come up with an approach they'll be interested in.

- Which nonprofit organizations have interests that are similar to yours? List them below:

1. _____

2. _____

3. _____

4. _____

5. _____

- How could you work your product into the heart of a sponsored PSA? List your ideas below for each nonprofit organization.

Organization: _____

1. _____

2. _____

# PSAs for Businesses

3. _____

4. _____

5. _____

Organization: _____

1. _____

2. _____

3. _____

4. _____

5. _____

Organization: _____

1. _____

2. _____

3. _____

4. _____

5. _____

Organization: _____

1. _____

2. _____

3. _____

4. _____

5. _____

Organization: _____

1. _____

2. _____

3. _____

4. _____

5. _____

- Now contact the publicists at these organizations and pitch your idea to them.

For related worksheets, see:

Checklist #40: Public Service Announcements
Checklist #41: Broadcasters' Policies for Public Service Announcements

# Part VI

# Working with the Media

Working with the media is the heart of any publicity program. The right approach to journalists will help ensure success, while the wrong approach can sabotage even the most powerful publicity concepts.

The checklists in this section will help you develop a forceful strategy for contacting the media by mail, telephone, fax, and EMail, and for handling even the most challenging follow-up contacts with journalists. The strategies you can develop using this section apply to newspapers, magazines, radio, television, and cable.

# 43

# Journalist Contact Preferences

Journalists have very strong preferences about how you contact them. At some publications, uninvited faxes are taboo and will kill a fantastic story on the spot. Other journalists love to get faxes but hate telephone calls. Fill in a copy of this worksheet for each journalist you work with (or want to work with). You may not learn all the journalist's preferences at first, but ask questions as you go along and record the answers.

Since journalists are often frantic at deadline time, never contact them then unless you have a major, breaking hard news story. If you know that a journalist's phone will be answered by voice mail, prepare a brief, 10- to 20-second pitch ahead of time and make sure it is so strong and enticing that the journalist will *have* to call you back. But also make sure you can deliver on that tantalizing promise.

If you're comfortable with computers, you can contact some journalists by electronic mail. It's ultrafast and inexpensive, but don't use it unless you are invited to. Still other journalists, particularly at magazines, may want stories submitted on disk. Find out what size disk and whether the journalist wants your story in a particular word-processing program format or in the universally readable ASCII (generic) format.

Dates this worksheet was updated: _____ _____ _____ _____

_____ _____ _____ _____

Media outlet name: _____

Journalist's name: _____

Address _____

_____

Phone: _____ Extension: _____

☐ Direct ☐ Switchboard ☐ Voice mail

After hours phone: _____

E-mail addresses: _____

Disk format/program for on-disk submissions: _____

Avoid calling at these times: _____

Needs _____ days/weeks lead time. Exceptions: _____

# Journalist Contact Preferences

| Contact Method | Prefers | OK | OK by Invitation | Never OK | Remarks |
|---|---|---|---|---|---|
| Telephone | | | | | |
| Regular US mail | | | | | |
| Express mail | | | | | |
| Federal Express | | | | | |
| E-mail | | | | | |
| On disk | | | | | |
| In person | | | | | |

For related worksheets, see:

Checklist #45: Telephoning Broadcast Journalists
Checklist #46: Contacting News Bureaus

# 44

# Telephone Contact Strategy Worksheet

Contacting journalists by telephone is an art. You have to come right to the point, make a persuasive pitch that grabs the reporter's interest, and then keep that interest. Always make sure that it's acceptable to call a journalist and that you are not calling at deadline time, unless you have a major breaking news story. Have your pitch ready, and have a purpose in mind. If this is a follow-up call and you have some interesting facts that weren't in your original material, let the journalist know that. Always keep a record of your calls and what you learned from them. Even seasoned publicists refine their craft on a daily basis, and writing down your experience helps you do that. In a typical initial telephone contact with a reporter, your goal is to tell the journalist what your news peg is in 10 seconds or less, and then find out the following:

- That you reached the right journalist for your story.

- That he or she is free to talk with you now.

- Whether he or she wants to talk about the story now or have you send, fax, or E-mail written material first.

You should make photocopies of this worksheet and fill out one for every telephone contact you plan to make.

Date: _____

Product/service: _____

Project: _____

Journalist to be called: _____

Purpose of call: _____

Follow-up action after call: _____

☐  I have verified that it is acceptable to call this journalist.

☐  I am avoiding this journalist's deadlines, which are: _____

This is

☐  an initial contact

☐  a follow-up call for materials sent on _____ .

☐  a follow-up call for an earlier contact on _____ .

# Telephone Contact Strategy

My main news peg is: _____

My alternate newspegs are: _____

_____

_____

My most interesting facts are:

1. _____

2. _____

3. _____

4. _____

Interesting facts I didn't include in the initial material are:

1. _____

2. _____

I'm prepared for

☐ direct, live contact with the journalist.

☐ voice mail.

☐ leaving a message with a receptionist.

Write a 10-second (maximum) pitch that states your news peg. Edit it until it is as concise as possible, then use a watch with a second hand to time it.

_____

_____

Record the results of your call below.

Results: _____

_____

What I learned: _____

_____

_____

# Telephone Contact Strategy

For related worksheets, see:

# 45

# Telephoning
# Broadcast Journalists

Since newscasters are under tremendous deadline pressure, you must come right to the point when you telephone them. Use this checklist to help you pitch your news stories to radio and television journalists. This format works best for events which have just recently happened.

1. Avoid calling journalists at deadline time unless you have major, breaking news.

2. Know which journalist will be interested in your story before you make your pitch.

3. Have the direct-dial numbers for broadcast newsrooms ready so you can get through to journalists after hours, when the switchboard is closed.

4. Assume that you are going to be taped whenever you call a broadcast journalist.

5. Sound professional and authoritative.

6. Be ready to state the essence of your story in 15 seconds or less. Practice this before you call.

7. Once you have told the journalist the substance of your story, ask if he or she wants to run a voice-level test. If he or she agrees, his or her equipment will be adjusted to tape your voice. This makes it more likely that he or she will use your material.

8. When the voice-level test is complete, restate the essence of your story. Then elaborate in 10- to 15-second sound bites with short pauses between them. You can read from a prepared script or a news release, provided you don't sound like you're reading. Practice until your delivery sounds like a natural speaking voice.

9. Be prepared for questions, and have your facts at hand.

10. If you notice that the reporter asks the same questions more than once, he or she is probably trying to get a briefer, more interesting, more quotable statement from you.

For related worksheets, see:

Checklist #36: Preparing News Releases for Broadcasters
Checklist #43: Journalist Contact Preferences
Checklist #44: Telephone Contact Strategy Worksheet

# 46 | Contacting News Bureaus

Contacting the local news bureaus of large circulation magazines and daily newspapers can help you build valuable working relationships with journalists that aren't as easy to develop if you approach the larger, more impersonal headquarters. If you make copies of this checklist and fill it out for every large publication you work with, your approach will be easier.

Date: _____

Publication name: _____

Does the publication have local bureaus you want to work with?

☐ Yes. Address: _____

      Telephone: _____

☐ I don't know. I'll have to call and ask or check a directory like *News Bureau Contacts*.

If this is a big city daily, have you checked to see if it has suburban bureaus?

☐ Yes

☐ Not yet

How does the publication want you to contact them?

☐ Headquarters only

☐ News bureaus only

What specialized reporters does the bureau have who would be interested in your organization's publicity?

Name _____ Specialty _____ Phone _____

Name _____ Specialty _____ Phone _____

Name _____ Specialty _____ Phone _____

Name _____ Specialty _____ Phone _____

Name _____ Specialty _____ Phone _____

Is the bureau staffed around the clock?

☐ No, the hours are: _____ to _____

    ☐ Monday through Friday  ☐ Daily

☐ Yes. The after-hours, direct-access telephone number is _____ .

# Contacting News Bureaus

Do your contacts at the bureau want faxed press releases?

☐ Yes, on breaking news only.

☐ Yes, under these conditions: _____

The fax number is: _____

☐ No, never.

Do your contacts at the bureau want E-mail press releases?

☐ Yes, on breaking news only.

☐ Yes, under these conditions: _____

Their E-mail addresses are:

_____        _____

_____        _____

☐ No, never.

# 47 Insuring Accurate Coverage

You can't control the media, but there *are* techniques you can use to help insure accuracy, especially in controversial circumstances or when technical information is involved. Follow these steps to get the best possible coverage:

1. Give the journalist detailed, written information when you make your first contact. Include in-depth backgrounder sheets in addition to your news release.

2. Make a list of common misconceptions about your product, service, organization, or cause, and your answers to these misconceptions. Give this list to the journalist when you make your first contact.

3. If you're concerned about unfavorable coverage, ask the reporter what negative statements he or she is likely to make. Then put your facts in order right on the spot, and counter the negative material with positive observations.

4. Ask the journalist if he or she will call you to read back direct quotes for accuracy. Sometimes this strategy works, but accept a refusal gracefully so you can go back to this journalist in the future.

5. Offer to review the technical information in a finished story for accuracy. Be sure to stick to a technical review of the facts. Not every journalist will take you up on this offer, but it's certainly worth trying.


For related worksheets, see:

Checklist #5: Using Misconceptions to Your Advantage
Checklist #10: Planning for Controversy
Checklist #17: Preparing Backgrounder Sheets

# Getting
# Photographic Coverage

There are two basic ways to get photographic coverage for a publicity story:

• Shoot the photos yourself, or

• Get the media outlet to send photographers or camera crews to an event.

The procedures in this Checklist work best for newspapers and television. If you are working with a magazine editor on a feature story, pitching the photos is part of pitching the story.

This Checklist takes you through the process of getting the media to give photo coverage to your event. For information on shooting photos yourself, see Checklist #38, Shooting Newsworthy Photos of People and Events.

Once you have chosen the media outlet you want to pitch for photographic coverage, fill in a separate Worksheet for each story you work on that calls for photographic coverage.

Date: _____

Product/service: _____

Project: _____

☐ Press conference  ☐ Event  ☐ Other

First make a list of possible media outlets for photo coverage.

1. Publication or broadcaster: _____

Does this media outlet use publicist-supplied photos?

☐ Yes  ☐ No

Does this media outlet have staff photographers or camera crews it will send to events?

☐ Yes  ☐ No

Assignment editor, photographic editor, or news editor who assigns photographers or camera crews:

Name: _____  Telephone: _____

Date called: _____  Results: _____

_____

Photo tip sheet sent on: _____  Follow-up call on: _____

Results: _____

# Photographic Coverage

2. Publication or broadcaster: _____

Does this media outlet use publicist-supplied photos?

☐ Yes  ☐ No

Does this media outlet have staff photographers or camera crews it will send to events?

☐ Yes  ☐ No

Assignment editor, photographic editor, or news editor who assigns photographers or camera crews:

Name: _____  Telephone: _____

Date called: _____  Results: _____

_____

Photo tip sheet sent on: _____  Follow-up call on: _____

Results: _____

3. Publication or broadcaster: _____

Does this media outlet use publicist-supplied photos?

☐ Yes  ☐ No

Does this media outlet have staff photographers or camera crews it will send to events?

☐ Yes  ☐ No

Assignment editor, photographic editor, or news editor who assigns photographers or camera crews:

Name: _____  Telephone: _____

Date called: _____  Results: _____

_____

Photo tip sheet sent on: _____  Follow-up call on: _____

Results: _____

4. Publication or broadcaster: _____

Does this media outlet use publicist-supplied photos?

☐ Yes  ☐ No

# Photographic Coverage

Does this media outlet have staff photographers or camera crews it will send to events?

☐ Yes ☐ No

Assignment editor, photographic editor, or news editor who assigns photographers or camera crews:

Name: _____ Telephone: _____

Date called: _____ Results: _____

_____

Photo tip sheet sent on: _____ Follow-up call on: _____

Results: _____

5. Publication or broadcaster: _____

Does this media outlet use publicist-supplied photos?

☐ Yes ☐ No

Does this media outlet have staff photographers or camera crews it will send to events?

☐ Yes ☐ No

Assignment editor, photographic editor, or news editor who assigns photographers or camera crews:

Name: _____ Telephone: _____

Date called: _____ Results: _____

_____

Photo tip sheet sent on: _____ Follow-up call on: _____

Results: _____

Now create a photo tip sheet and send it to the photo editors, news editors, or assignment editors. You can also include it with your news conference or special event invitations.

1. At the top of your tip sheet list the following:
   • Your organization's name
   • Your address
   • Your telephone number
   • Media contact's name
   • Media contact's telephone number

2. Include the words "photo opportunity" in large type.

3. Give the following critical information about the event:

   - Date

   - Day

   - Time

   - Address

   - Location at the address

   - Telephone number that will be answered on the day of the event by someone familiar with the event

   - Purpose of the event

4. Summarize the event in 15 to 20 words.

5. List the photo possibilities one by one. Include the time each is happening.

Never assume that the photographers or camera crews who arrive at your event have been well briefed. Have at least one person assigned to meet and greet them, give them background information, and help them in any way they need. Extra copies of your photo tip sheet will be very helpful to them, so have some ready.

For related worksheets, see:

Checklist #32: Hiring a News Photograher
Checklist #33: Technical Requirements for News Photos
Checklist #34: Shooting Newsworthy Photos of People and Events
Checklist #35: Product Photography

# Following Up on News Releases

When it comes to following up on news releases, there is a basic conflict of interest. Most journalists don't want you to bother them. But you know that journalists are human and may forget about your release. You can solve this dilemma by reminding them without annoying them. One word of warning: Never do this at journalists' deadline times! They won't have time to discuss anything but breaking news then. After you are certain enough time has passed for the news release to be delivered, follow the steps in this worksheet:

Date: _____

Product/service: _____

Project: _____

1. Write a ten-second summary of your release.

   _____

   _____

2. List two or three fascinating, compelling, and interesting facts that weren't included in your news release. You may even want to plan your news releases so you always have this "extra" material.

   _____

   _____

   _____

3. Call the journalist and provide the following information:

   • Your name and organization's name

   • Some new information you didn't include in your release and a quick summary of the release

4. Ask if he or she wants to write down the new information, and then be brief and to the point.

5. If the journalist can't remember or can't find your release, don't get upset. You may have created a first-rate opportunity here: Focus on that! Offer to mail, hand-deliver, or fax another copy of the release to him or her, and then do it immediately.

For related worksheets, see:

Checklist #14: Selecting Newsworthy Facts
Checklist #21: Writing and Editing News Releases
Checklist #23: Meeting the Needs of Broadcast Journalists

# Following Up News Releases

# 50 Following Up Press Conferences and Special Events

Unless you have major, breaking news, some journalists may not be able to attend your media event. But they may cover it anyway, if you follow up the event or conference with solid, newsworthy material they can use to produce a story. Use this checklist to help you follow up for maximum media coverage after a media event.

1. Write a 7- to 15-second summary of the news announced at your event.

2. Call reporters who did not attend to brief them with this summary. Let them know that your media kit or other material is on the way and when it will arrive. Ask them if that's soon enough; if it isn't, arrange to get the material there sooner.

3. Include photographs in your follow-up materials whenever possible.

4. If you're calling radio news directors, ask if they want to run a voice-level test first. If they agree, they will record your statement for possible use on the air.

5. Ask them if there is anything else they need from you.

6. Never mention how many journalists attended the event. Even if nobody covered it, you must be positive and refer to the newsworthy information. There have been media events that no journalists attended, but they still received coverage as a result of good follow-up work by publicists.

7. Send your media kit to every reporter who did not attend your event. Use a messenger service to meet deadlines if necessary.

8. Write a one- to two-page news release based on what your speakers said and include it with your media kit.

9. Have the telephone number on your media invitation staffed during the event. Check in after the event to see if any journalists called for information. If they did, get it to them immediately.

10. If you have the budget, record your media event on broadcast-quality video or audiotape and send it to broadcasters who couldn't cover the event in person.

11. Even better, have your tape edited into a video news release (see Checklist #24) or the equivalent for radio, and send that instead. But be certain you can make journalists' deadlines. Journalists who did not attend will be less likely to run your story if their competitors who attended have already covered it.

For related worksheets, see:

Checklist #11: Staffing the Telephone
Checklist #12: Planning Press Conferences and Special Events
Checklist #21: Writing and Editing News Releases
Checklist #24: Creating the Video News Release Concept
Checklist #43: Journalist Contact Preferences
Checklist #44: Telephone Contact Strategy Worksheet
Checklist #45: Telephoning Boadcast Journalists
Checklist #46: Contacting News Bureaus

# Part VII

# Using Outside Resources

Outside resources are often essential for researching, producing, and distributing publicity materials. The checklists in this section will help you evaluate and choose computer database services, production houses, fax distribution services, and clipping services, and develop budgets for outside services on a project-by-project basis.

# 51

# Using Computer Databases for Research

Computer databases can be a highly efficient tool for researching what's been said in the media about your organization, your industry, your competition, your product, or your cause. You can also gather information that will help you create news pegs and backgrounder sheets. But you need to know in advance approximately what it will cost you to use a database and how you'll learn to use it. Fill out a separate copy of this worksheet for every database you're considering.

Date: _____

Database name: _____

1. How will you learn to use this database?

   ☐ A training session offered by the database operator

   ☐ A third-party training session

   ☐ On-line help

   ☐ On-line practice sessions or tutorials

   ☐ How-to material I can access on-line and download

   ☐ A how-to book: _____

   ☐ Other _____

2. How much will it cost to use this database?

   A. Membership fee ☐ yearly ☐ quarterly ☐ monthly $ _____

   B. Initiation fee $ _____

   C. Cost of software $ _____

   D. Other $ _____

   E. Monthly fee $ _____

   F. Estimated hours of use per month _____

   G. Telephone company charges for connect time per hour $ _____

      This amount times estimated hours use per month $ _____

   H. Timesharing service charges for connect time per hour $ _____

      This amount times estimated hours use per month $ _____

# Using Computer Databases

    I.  Hourly charge for accessing the database per hour     $ _____

        This amount times estimated hours usage per month     $ _____

        Extra surcharge for high-speed modems     $ _____

    J.  Hourly surcharges for specialized areas of the database per hour     $ _____

        This amount times estimated hours usage per month     $ _____

    K. Per item surcharges for searching, printing out, and other "extra" services     $ _____

        Searching     $ _____

        This amount times estimated monthly usage     $ _____

        Printing out     $ _____

        This amount times estimated monthly usage     $ _____

        Other _____     $ _____

        This amount times estimated monthly usage     $ _____

    L. Other recurring fees

        _____     $ _____

        _____     $ _____

    M. How many searches do you expect to do monthly? _____

Is it more cost effective to do the database searches yourself or to have a search service do them for you? Here's how to make a rough estimate:

1.  Add up your start-up costs for using this database (Items A+B+C+D) and enter
    the result here:     $ _____

2.  Add up your monthly usage fees (Items E, G, H, I, J, K, L) and enter the result here:     $ _____

    Multiply by 12     $ _____

3.  Add 1 and 2 and enter result here:     $ _____

4.  Multiply the number of searches you expect to do in a month by 12 and enter
    the result here:     _____

5.  Divide result 3 by result 4 and enter here:     $ _____

    This is your cost per search. Compare this cost with the fees charged by database search services.

# 52

# Press Clipping Services

Press clipping services and on-line databases can show you the immediate results of your publicity, but you have to evaluate them before you start using them. This worksheet will help you decide which service(s) to use and estimate how much they'll cost. You should fill out a copy of this worksheet for each service you are considering.

Date: _____

Service name: _____

This is a

☐ service.  ☐ on-line database.

Can they evaluate your clippings?

☐ Yes  ☐ No

If this is a database, do they have full-text articles or are they limited to summaries of your key publications? A database that does not have full-text articles will have limited usefulness for you. If this is a clipping service, make sure they read your key publications. List your key publications below, and check with the database or service to find out the status of each publication.

| Publication Name | Full Text | Summary Only | Read | Not Read or Carried |
|---|---|---|---|---|
| _____ | _____ | _____ | _____ | _____ |
| _____ | _____ | _____ | _____ | _____ |
| _____ | _____ | _____ | _____ | _____ |
| _____ | _____ | _____ | _____ | _____ |
| _____ | _____ | _____ | _____ | _____ |
| _____ | _____ | _____ | _____ | _____ |
| _____ | _____ | _____ | _____ | _____ |
| _____ | _____ | _____ | _____ | _____ |
| _____ | _____ | _____ | _____ | _____ |
| _____ | _____ | _____ | _____ | _____ |
| _____ | _____ | _____ | _____ | _____ |

# Press Clipping Services

| Publication Name | Full Text | Summary Only | Read | Not Read or Carried |
|---|---|---|---|---|
| _____ | \_\_\_\_ | \_\_\_\_ | \_\_\_\_ | \_\_\_\_ |
| _____ | \_\_\_\_ | \_\_\_\_ | \_\_\_\_ | \_\_\_\_ |
| _____ | \_\_\_\_ | \_\_\_\_ | \_\_\_\_ | \_\_\_\_ |
| _____ | \_\_\_\_ | \_\_\_\_ | \_\_\_\_ | \_\_\_\_ |
| _____ | \_\_\_\_ | \_\_\_\_ | \_\_\_\_ | \_\_\_\_ |
| _____ | \_\_\_\_ | \_\_\_\_ | \_\_\_\_ | \_\_\_\_ |

Geographic area covered:

☐ Local   ☐ Regional   ☐ National   ☐ International

Number of publications read or included:

Daily papers: _____      Weekly papers: _____

Consumer magazines: _____      Trade magazines: _____

Newsletters: _____      Other _____

Number of broadcast transcripts available:

Large metro-area television: _____      Large metro-area radio: _____

Other \_\_ _____

In order to find the articles and materials you want, you'll have to enter or supply key words that best describe them. List the key words you'll need to use with this service or database below:

| | | |
|---|---|---|
| _____ | _____ | _____ |
| _____ | _____ | _____ |
| _____ | _____ | _____ |
| _____ | _____ | _____ |
| _____ | _____ | _____ |
| _____ | _____ | _____ |
| _____ | _____ | _____ |

# Press Clipping Services

## Clipping Service Fees

Monthly membership/minimum fee     $ _____

Per clipping fee $_____ × estimated number of clippings per month     $ _____

Mounting fee $_____ × estimated number of clippings per month     $ _____

Postage and handling fee     $ _____

Estimated monthly total     $ _____

## Database fees

1. Enter all the monthly fees from Checklist #52: Using Computer Databases for Research that apply to maintaining a clipping portfolio on this database:     $ _____

2. Enter the per-clipping fee, including downloading or print-out fees, if any:     $ _____

3. Multiply the estimated number of clippings per month by line 2:
   _____ (estimated number of clippings) × _____ (per clipping fee) =     $ _____

4. Add monthly fees (line 1) and clipping fees (line 3) to get your estimated cost per month to use this service:     $ _____

For related worksheets, see:

Checklist #51: Using Computer Databases for Research

# 53 Choosing a Faxed News Release Distribution Service

The Securities and Exchange Commission (SEC) has strict regulations that publicly traded companies must meet when they distribute news stories that could impact their stock prices. Publicists must make sure that all investors will have the opportunity to act on the news at the same time, so nobody has an unfair advantage. Because of this timely notification requirement, the overwhelming majority of financial publicists use fax services or news wires to distribute their news stories. Because you are required to deliver your news to a number of media outlets simultaneously, you can't use an ordinary fax machine. This table gives the criteria you should use when you choose a faxed news release distribution service. Fill out a copy of this worksheet for each service you evaluate.

| Critical Questions | Acceptable | Unacceptable |
|---|---|---|
| How many faxes can they transmit simultaneously? | More than your media list | Less than your media list |
| What is the longest waiting time for transmittal? | 5 minutes | More than 5 minutes |
| Can they store your letter head and signature in their computer? | Yes | No |
| How many times will they retry a busy fax number? | Multiple | None |
| How will they handle a situation where the recipient can't be faxed? | Phone calls to the recipient and you | Nothing |
| Will they store and maintain your client contact lists in their computer? | Yes | No |
| How much time is needed to make changes to this list? | Minutes | Days or hours |

## Additional Questions

How many outgoing lines do they have? _____

How many clients do they have? _____

Will they supply client references? _____

Has a client ever had an SEC problem that was attributed to this fax service? If so, what was it? _____

_____

How do they confirm that your faxes were received? _____

Do they provide you with copies of these confirmations? _____

Can they generate cover pages that let recipients
know which person in their organization this fax is for? _____

# Faxed News Release Distribution Services

Can you fax them material to be faxed? _____

How will they insure the image they receive will be clear enough for retransmission?_____

Can you upload material to be faxed from your PC using a modem? _____

Is there a set-up fee?

☐ Yes, _____     ☐ No

Are there minimum charges?

☐ Yes, _____     ☐ No

Do they supply a daily accounting of on-line time billed?

☐ Yes   ☐ No


For related worksheets, see:

Checklist #58: Disclosure for Publicly Traded Companies

# 54 The Right Production House for Your Video News Release

Video news releases (VNRs) require an investment of between $15,000 and $30,000. The return on this investment depends on the expertise of the production house you work with. Use this checklist to help you evaluate each production house you are considering.

Name of production house: _____

Contact: _____

Address: _____

Telephone: _____ Fax: _____

Recommended by: _____

1. How long have they been in business? _____

2. How many VNRs have they produced? _____

3. What is their Dun & Bradstreet rating? _____

4 . Have they received any creative awards or honors? If so, list them. _____

_____

5. Who is on their client list?

_____     _____

_____     _____

_____     _____

_____     _____

6. Who are their references?

Company name: _____

Contact name: _____

Telephone: _____

How much airplay did their VNR receive? _____

Reference's remarks: _____

_____

# Right Production House/Video News Release

Company name: _____

Contact name: _____

Telephone: _____

How much airplay did their VNR receive? _____

Reference's remarks: _____

_____

Company name: _____

Contact name: _____

Telephone: _____

How much airplay did their VNR receive? _____

Reference's remarks: _____

_____

Company name: _____

Contact name: _____

Telephone: _____

How much airplay did their VNR receive? _____

Reference's remarks: _____

_____

7. How many seasoned television people are on their staff? _____

8. What are their names, titles, and television experience?

| Name | Title | TV experience |
|---|---|---|
| _____ | _____ | _____ |
| _____ | _____ | _____ |
| _____ | _____ | _____ |

9. Is all of their equipment broadcast quality?

☐ Yes. ☐ No. Explain: _____

10. Can they guarantee they'll meet media deadlines, particularly with breaking news?

    ☐ Yes  ☐ No

11. Do they have a full-time station relations staff?

    ☐ Yes  ☐ No

12. If they don't have a full-time station relations staff, will they be comfortable working with one of the larger video houses that also distributes VNRs and does have this staff?

    ☐ Yes  ☐ No

13. How often do they update their media contact database? (If this is not done monthly or more frequently, you'll waste money sending VNRs to outdated contacts.)

    ☐ Monthly  ☐ Weekly  ☐ Daily  ☐ Other _____

14. What types of information does their media contact database include?

    _____     _____

    _____     _____

    _____     _____

    _____     _____

15. Can they distribute or arrange to distribute your VNR by satellite?

    ☐ Yes  ☐ No

16. How does satellite distribution compare in cost to mail distribution?

    ☐ The same

    ☐ $ _____ less

    ☐ $ _____ more

17. What exactly is included in their contract?

    _____     _____

    _____     _____

    _____     _____

    _____     _____

_____     _____

_____     _____

_____     _____

_____     _____

18. What exactly is *not* included in their contract?

_____     _____

_____     _____

_____     _____

_____     _____

_____     _____

_____     _____

_____     _____

19. Under what conditions will there be extra or overtime charges?

_____     _____

_____     _____

_____     _____

_____     _____

_____     _____

_____     _____

_____     _____

For related worksheets, see:

Checklist #13: Video Production Approvals
Checklist #24: Creating the Video News Release Concept
Checklist #36: Preparing News Releases for Broadcasters
Checklist #37: Technical Requirements for Video News Releases

# 55

# The Right Production House for Your Satellite Media Tour

Satellite media tours (SMTs) require a large investment. The return on this investment depends on the expertise of the production house you work with. Use this checklist to help you evaluate each production house you are considering.

Name of production house: _____

Contact: _____

Address: _____

Telephone: _____ Fax: _____

Recommended by: _____

1. How long have they been in business? _____

2. How many SMTs have they produced? _____

3. What is their Dun & Bradstreet rating? _____ _____

4. Who is on their client list?

   _____ _____     _____ _____

   _____ _____     _____ _____

   _____                     _____

   _____                     _____

5. Who are their references?

   Company name: _____

   Contact name: _____

   Telephone: _____

   How much airplay did their SMT receive? _____

   Reference's remarks: _____

   _____

# Right Production House/Satellite Media Tour

Company name: _____

Contact name: _____

Telephone: _____

How much airplay did their SMT receive? _____

Reference's remarks: _____

_____

Company name: _____

Contact name: _____

Telephone: _____

How much airplay did their SMT receive? _____

Reference's remarks: _____

_____

Company name: _____

Contact name: _____

Telephone: _____

How much airplay did their SMT receive? _____

Reference's remarks: _____

_____

6. How many seasoned television people are on their staff?_____

7. What are their names, titles, and experience?

| Name | Title | Television experience |
|------|-------|----------------------|
| _____ | _____ | _____ |
| _____ | _____ | _____ |
| _____ | _____ | _____ |

8. Is all of their equipment broadcast quality?

☐ Yes.　☐ No. Explain: _____

9. Can they guarantee they'll meet media deadlines, particularly with breaking news?

   ☐ Yes ☐ No

10. Do they have a full-time station relations staff?

    ☐ Yes

    ☐ No. How do they handle station relations? _____

11. How often do they update their media contact database? (If this is not done monthly or more frequently, you'll waste money sending VNRs to outdated contacts.)

    ☐ Monthly ☐ Weekly ☐ Daily ☐ Other _____

12. What types of information does their media contact database include?

    _____    _____

    _____    _____

    _____    _____

    _____    _____

13. Do they own their studio or rent it?

    ☐ Own ☐ Rent

14. Can you visit their studio and watch an SMT in progress before you sign the contract?

    ☐ Yes ☐ No

    ☐ Arranged for date/time: _____

15. Do they own or rent the uplink facilities?

    ☐ Own ☐ Rent

16. What exactly is included in their contract?

    _____    _____

    _____    _____

    _____    _____

    _____    _____

    _____    _____

_____     _____

_____     _____

_____     _____

17. What exactly is *not* included in their contract?

_____     _____

_____     _____

_____     _____

_____     _____

_____     _____

_____     _____

18. Under what conditions will there be extra or overtime charges?

_____     _____

_____     _____

_____     _____

_____     _____

_____     _____

_____     _____

19. The bottom line is: do you trust the operator enough so you'll feel comfortable standing clear during the tour?

☐ Yes   ☐ No (This is a warning sign! You probably should choose another operator.)

For related worksheets, see:

Checklist #26: Planning Satellite Media Tours

# Part VIII

# Legal and Ethical Issues

Every publicity activity you engage in has legal implications. Aside from the Securities and Exchange Commission regulations that apply to publicly traded companies, you will have to consider the statutes and regulations governing contracts, copyright, trade names, fair trade, lobbying, permits, libel, and more.

Most lawyers do not have a thorough grasp of the everyday operations of an active, successful publicity program, so you can't rely on them to see every legal pitfall in advance. Even the best lawyer needs a thorough, organized explanation of your publicity program's activities.

The checklists in this section will help you brief your legal counsel about your publicity program so he or she can help you avoid problems. They will also help you create permanent records of sources of information and quotes as well as approvals, so you will be prepared if legal action is brought against your organization in the future.

Even if you follow the letter of the law, that may not be enough. Publicity must also withstand public scrutiny, or you will alienate journalists and your audience and render yourself ineffective no matter how large your budget may be. This section will help you anticipate and avoid potential problems with ethical issues and public scrutiny.

56. Legal Aspects of Publicity
57. Protecting Yourself
58. Disclosure for Publicly Traded Companies
59. Withstanding Public Scrutiny

# Legal Aspects of Publicity

It may surprise you that even simple publicity activities may have legal implications. This worksheet will help you organize information to present to your lawyer, so he or she can review your publicity program and counsel you. Since every situation is different, the form can't be complete, so be sure you tell your lawyer about everything you're doing and plan to do. It's also a good idea to save this worksheet. If any legal questions arise at a later date, you will have a record of your attorney's response to your questions.

Date: _____

Review this worksheet again on: _____ (Enter this date in your appointment book.)

Name of attorney consulted: _____

1. Could anyone make a case that your publicity material is designed to influence legislation?

    ☐ Yes.

    _____ I have checked with our organization's lawyer, and we don't need to register as lobbyists

    because _____

    ☐ Our attorney advises us to register as a lobbyist, and we have taken the following steps to

    comply:

    Action: _____ Date: _____

    Action: _____ Date: _____

    Action: _____ Date: _____

    Action: _____ Date: _____

    Action: _____ Date: _____

    Action: _____ Date: _____

    ☐ No.
    Have you checked your opinion with your supervisor and other executives in your organization?
    Write their names and dates here:

    Name: _____ Date: _____

    Name: _____ Date: _____

    Name: _____ Date: _____

    Name: _____ Date: _____

# Legal Aspects of Publicity

2. If your company is publicly traded, will any of your publicity releases have an impact on your organization's stock prices?

☐ Yes.

    ☐ I have checked with our organization's lawyer, and we don't need to meet Securities and Exchange Commission guidelines for timely distribution because _____

_____

    ☐ We need to comply on all releases.

    ☐ We need to comply on the following types of releases only:

    _____    _____

    _____    _____

    _____    _____

    _____    _____

    _____    _____

    _____    _____

☐ No.
Have you checked your opinion with your supervisor and other executives in your organization? Write their names and dates here:

Name: _____    Date: _____

Name: _____    Date: _____

Name: _____    Date: _____

Name: _____    Date: _____

3. Do you ever hold press conferences and special events, or shoot video news releases and satellite media tours in public locations?

☐ Yes.

    ☐ We *do not need* permits for press conferences, special events, video news release shoots, and satellite media tour shoots in the following locations, according to our attorney:

    _____    _____

    _____    _____

    _____    _____

# Legal Aspects of Publicity

_____     _____

_____     _____

_____     _____

☐ We *do need* permits for press conferences, special events, video news release shoots, and satellite media tour shoots in the following locations, according to our attorney. I have noted this on my master copy of the worksheets for these activities:

_____     _____

_____     _____

_____     _____

_____     _____

4. Make a list of the types of freelance and subcontract help you use in your publicity program. Then indicate whether you use contracts, and what changes your attorney recommends when she reviews them.

| Type of Help | Contract Used? | Contract Needed? | Attorney's Recommendations |
|---|---|---|---|
| Photographers | _____ | _____ | _____ |
| Writers | _____ | _____ | _____ |
| Mailing house | _____ | _____ | _____ |
| Audio production house | _____ | _____ | _____ |
| Video production house | _____ | _____ | _____ |
| _____ | _____ | _____ | _____ |
| _____ | _____ | _____ | _____ |
| _____ | _____ | _____ | _____ |

# Legal Aspects of Publicity

5. Have you reviewed with your attorney what you can and can't say about litigation involving your organization?

☐ Yes. We cannot say the following about matters in litigation:

_____

_____

_____

_____

☐ No. That doesn't apply to us.
Have you checked your opinion with your supervisor and other executives in your organization? Write their names and dates here:

Name: _____ Date: _____

Name: _____ Date: _____

Name: _____ Date: _____

Name: _____ Date: _____

6. Has your attorney reviewed your organization's emergency publicity and media relations plan?

☐ Yes. He or she recommends the following changes:

Change needed: _____ Action taken: _____

Change needed: _____ Action taken: _____

Change needed: _____ Action taken: _____

Change needed: _____ Action taken: _____

Change needed: _____ Action taken: _____

Change needed: _____ Action taken: _____

☐ No. That doesn't apply to us.
Have you checked your opinion with your supervisor and other executives in your organization? Write their names and dates here:

Name: _____ Date: _____

Name: _____ Date: _____

Name: _____ Date: _____

Name: _____ Date: _____

7. Can your attorney provide legal support and input in emergencies and disasters?

☐ Yes. He or she will do that in the following situations:

_____

_____

_____

_____

☐ No. That doesn't apply to us.
Have you checked your opinion with your supervisor and other executives in your organization? Write their names and dates here:

Name: _____ Date: _____

Name: _____ Date: _____

Name: _____ Date: _____

Name: _____ Date: _____

For related worksheets, see:

Checklist #57: Protecting Yourself
Checklist #58: Disclosure for Publicly Traded Companies
Checklist #59: Withstanding Public Scrutiny

# 57

# Protecting Yourself

To do a good job as a publicist, you must keep a high profile, and you may have to defend your work months or years after you finish a project. A few simple procedures can help you protect yourself from unwarranted criticism. Use a copy of this worksheet to keep a record for every project you do, and if a problem arises later, you'll have a written record to fall back on.

Date: _____

Product/service: _____

Project: _____

1. Do you really believe there's a newsworthy story here?

   ☐ Yes.

   ☐ No. Explain why you're doing this project even though you don't believe it's newsworthy.

   _____

   _____

   Have you tried to develop another peg that's more newsworthy?

   ☐ Yes. Results: _____

   ☐ No. Explain: _____

2. The information in this publicity material comes from _____

   _____

   _____

   _____

   _____

   ☐ My notes are attached

   ☐ My notes are filed under _____

   ☐ Source memos are attached

   ☐ Source memos are filed under _____

# Protecting Yourself

3. Make a list of the interviews and conversations on which you based this publicity, and where your notes and confirming memos are filed.

| Date | Interview With | Follow-Up Memo Sent | Follow-Up Memo Filed | Notes Filed |
|------|----------------|---------------------|----------------------|-------------|
| _____ | _____ | _____ | _____ | _____ |
| _____ | _____ | _____ | _____ | _____ |
| _____ | _____ | _____ | _____ | _____ |
| _____ | _____ | _____ | _____ | _____ |
| _____ | _____ | _____ | _____ | _____ |
| _____ | _____ | _____ | _____ | _____ |
| _____ | _____ | _____ | _____ | _____ |
| _____ | _____ | _____ | _____ | _____ |
| _____ | _____ | _____ | _____ | _____ |

4. Make a list of the approvals you got for this publicity from others in your organization, what format those approvals took (memos, initials, and so on) and where you filed those approvals.

| Date | From | For | Format | Filed |
|------|------|-----|--------|-------|
| _____ | _____ | _____ | _____ | _____ |
| _____ | _____ | _____ | _____ | _____ |
| _____ | _____ | _____ | _____ | _____ |
| _____ | _____ | _____ | _____ | _____ |
| _____ | _____ | _____ | _____ | _____ |
| _____ | _____ | _____ | _____ | _____ |
| _____ | _____ | _____ | _____ | _____ |
| _____ | _____ | _____ | _____ | _____ |
| _____ | _____ | _____ | _____ | _____ |

5. Make a list of the quotes you used in this material and how you verified those quotes for accuracy.

| Date | Person Quoted | Verified | Type of Verification | Filed |
|------|---------------|----------|----------------------|-------|
| _____ | _____ | _____ | _____ | _____ |
| _____ | _____ | _____ | _____ | _____ |
| _____ | _____ | _____ | _____ | _____ |
| _____ | _____ | _____ | _____ | _____ |
| _____ | _____ | _____ | _____ | _____ |
| _____ | _____ | _____ | _____ | _____ |
| _____ | _____ | _____ | _____ | _____ |
| _____ | _____ | _____ | _____ | _____ |
| _____ | _____ | _____ | _____ | _____ |
| _____ | _____ | _____ | _____ | _____ |

For related worksheets, see:

Checklist #1:   Defining Your Authority
Checklist #56:  Legal Aspects of Publicity
Checklist #58:  Disclosure for Publicly Traded Companies
Checklist #59: Withstanding Public Scrutiny

# 58 Disclosure for Publicly Traded Companies

The Securities and Exchange Commission (SEC) has strict regulations that publicly traded companies must meet when they distribute news stories that could impact their stock prices. Publicists must make sure that all investors will have the opportunity to act on the news at the same time, so nobody has an unfair advantage. Because of this timely notification requirement, the overwhelming majority of financial publicists use fax services or news wires to distribute their news stories. But even if you don't handle financial publicity per se, if your story could impact stock prices, disclosure requirements apply to you, too. For each news story you release, fill in a copy of this worksheet and file it away safely in case there is ever a question. If the SEC decides to investigate your compliance with disclosure regulations five years from now, you'll have some very helpful records.

Date: _____

Product/service: _____

Project: _____

1. Is there any conceivable way this story could impact your organization's stock prices?

☐ Yes. Disclosure is needed.

☐ No, because _____

_____

_____

_____

_____

2. If you answered no to Question 1, have you discussed your opinion with anyone else?

☐ Yes (list below)

Name: _____ Title: _____

Date: _____ Remarks: _____

Name: _____ Title: _____

Date: _____ Remarks: _____

Name: _____ Title: _____

Date: _____ Remarks: _____

Name: _____ Title: _____

Date: _____ Remarks: _____

# Disclosure of Companies

☐ No

3. If you answered yes to question 1, disclosure is needed. Complete the following:

This release was simultaneously sent to the following media outlets by

☐ _____ fax service

☐ _____ wire service

☐ _____ other

Date: _____ Time: _____

**Required Media Outlets**

☐ Dow Jones News Service

☐ Reuters

☐ Moody's

☐ *The New York Times*

☐ *The Wall Street Journal*

☐ Standard & Poor's

☐ Associated Press

☐ United Press International

**Other Media Outlets**

☐ List Attached

☐ _____

☐ _____

☐ _____

☐ _____

☐ _____

☐ _____

☐ _____

For related worksheets, see:

Checklist #53: Choosing a Faxed News Release Distribution Service
Checklist #56: Legal Aspects of Publicity

# Withstanding Public Scrutiny

You should review every piece of publicity material before you send it out to make sure it will withstand public scrutiny. If it can't, you can do considerable damage to your organization's reputation—and your bottom line—if the media decide to investigate spurious claims.

Ask yourself the following questions about each publicity item:

- Is there anything in this piece that my lawyer should see before I send it out?

- Are there any significant facts that I have not included here? Have I given journalists the complete picture?

- Will anyone feel that I have "pulled a fast one" by omitting facts?

- Is there anyone in the media's audience who might object to or question the statements in this material?

- If there is, am I prepared to answer their objections with factual material?

- Can I support the facts in this material with evidence if they are questioned?

- Would I be comfortable attesting to the facts in this publicity material under oath?

If you can't answer these questions appropriately, revise the piece or don't send it out.

For related worksheets, see:

Checklist #56: Legal Aspects of Publicity
Checklist #57: Protecting Yourself